DATE DUE   JAN 04

vyos

AR 04 04			
2-13-07			
8-31-13			
9-12-13			
105-13			
GAYLORD			PRINTED IN U.S.A.

Dave Barry's Bad Habits

Dave Barry's Bad Habits
A 100% Fact-Free Book

DAVE BARRY

BEELER LARGE PRINT
Hampton Falls, New Hampshire, 2003

Library of Congress Cataloging-in-Publication Data

Barry, Dave.
    Dave Barry's bad habits : a 100% fact free book / Dave
Barry.
            p.   cm.
        ISBN 1-57490-524-4 (lg. print : alk. paper)
        1. American wit and humor. 2. Large type books. I. Title:
Bad habits. II. Title.

    PN6162.B295 2003
    814'.54—dc22   2003018207

Published in Large Print by arrangement with
Doubleday Books, a division of Random House, Inc.

BEELER LARGE PRINT
is published by
Thomas T. Beeler, Publisher
Post Office Box 659
Hampton Falls, New Hampshire 03844

Typeset in 16 point Times New Roman type.
Sewn and bound on acid-free paper by
Sheridan Books in Chelsea, Michigan

To Mom and Dad,
who never forced me to go see Santa Claus

Dave Barry's Bad Habits

Contents

The Media Is the Mess-up

Low Finance

Health Habits

Culture Staggers On

A Little Learning . . .

Scientific Stuff

Eat, Drink, and Be Wary

Traveling Light

The Sporting Life

Tips from the Bottom

Introduction

WHEN PEOPLE COME to my home for the first time, they often ask me, "Dave, where's the bathroom?" To which I always answer, "Down the hall there, on the left." And from that point on we are usually close friends.

I bring this up because people often wonder what I'm really like. "Dave," they often ask, when they get out of the bathroom, "are you really as witty, insightful, articulate, and handsome as your writing suggests?" I would have to say that yes, I am, although I am not as tall as you might think. I'm maybe five nine. But then a lot of truly great writers were of average height or less. William Shakespeare was only fifteen inches tall!

Which leads us to accuracy. When Doubleday & Company decided, after days of heavy drinking, to publish this book, they hired a panel of extremely brilliant nuclear physicists, who combed through these essays and marked, with a red pencil, every sentence that might conceivably be accurate, and these sentences were all removed with pruning shears. So I freely admit, right up front, that there are no facts left in this book, and I don't want you Little League coaches out there to send me a lot of cretin letters informing me that a ten-year-old can't really throw a baseball six hundred miles an hour. Okay?

So there you have it, except for my philosophy of life. My mother used to say to me: "Son, it's better to be rich and healthy than poor and sick." I think that still makes a heck of a lot of sense, even in these troubled times.

Household Perils

It's in the Genes

MY WIFE AND I were both born without whatever brain part it is that enables people to decorate their homes. If we had lived in the Neanderthal era, ours would be the only cave without little drawings of elk on the walls.

When we moved into our house eight years ago, there was this lighting fixture in the dining room that obviously had been installed by vandals. Simply removing this fixture would be too good for it; this is the kind of fixture that needs to be taken out in the backyard and shot. When people came over to visit, back when we first moved in, we'd gesture toward the fixture derisively and say, "Of course *that's* got to go."

Of course we still have it. We have no way of deciding what to replace it with. What we *have* done is get an electrician to come in and move the fixture to another part of the dining room, because, after years of thinking about it with our defective brains, we thought this might be a good decorative idea. To move the fixture, the electrician had to punch holes, some of them big enough to put your fist through, in the wall and ceiling. I have taped plastic sandwich bags over these holes, to keep the air from rushing in and out.

So now, after eight years, we have the original vandal fixture, *plus* we have holes with plastic bags over them. We eat in the kitchen. We will always eat in the kitchen, and our dining room will always look like the South Bronx. We have learned that anything we try to do to improve it will just make it worse, because of these missing brain parts.

We do a lot of work with plastic bags. We made

curtains for several rooms by taping up dark plastic garbage bags. My wife feels guilty about this, because she believes women are supposed to have this Betty Crocker gland somewhere that secretes a hormone that enables them to sew curtains. God knows she has tried. She reads articles, she takes measurements, she even goes to the fabric store, but because of what she perceives to be a deficiency of her Betty Crocker gland, she never actually produces any curtains. Which is fine, because I have a deficiency of my Mr. Goodwrench gland and would never put them up.

So we use plastic garbage bags. They work fine, but I have noticed that most of our friends, now that we're all grown-ups, have switched over to actual cloth curtains. Also they have tasteful Danish furniture. They just went out and got it somehow, as if it were no big deal, and now everything matches, like those photographs in snotty interior design magazines featuring homes owned by wealthy people who eat out and keep their children in Switzerland. We have this green armchair we got at an auction for twenty-five cents. This is not one of those chairs that are sold for a song but turn out to be tasteful antiques worth thousands of dollars. This chair, at twenty-five cents, was clearly overpriced. It looks, from a distance, like a wad of mucus, and it could not possibly match any other furniture because any furniture that looked like it would have been burned years ago.

Accompanying this chair is a sofa that some people we know tried to throw away six years ago, which we have covered with a blanket to prevent guests from looking directly at it and being blinded or driven insane. Such is the tastelessness of this sofa. And these are two of our better pieces. The only really nice furniture we own is manufactured by the Fisher-Price toy company for my son's little Fisher-Price people, although I certainly don't begrudge them that, inasmuch as they have no arms or legs.

I imagine you're going to suggest that we go out and buy a nice piece of furniture, and then, when we can afford it, another one, and so on until we have a regular grown-up neat and tasteful home. This would never work. If we were to put a nice piece of furniture in our living room, all the other furniture would wait until we'd gone to bed, then ridicule and deride the new furniture, and emit all kinds of shabbiness germs into the living room atmosphere, and by morning the new furniture would be old and stained and hideous. I also firmly believe that if we were to leave our chair in one of our friends' tasteful living rooms four several days, it would become sleek and Danish.

This interior decorating problem extends to cars. None of my friends, for example, have plaster models of their teeth in their cars. I have two in my car. My dentist gives them to me from time to time, sort of like a treat, and I'm afraid to throw them away for fear he'll get angry and make me come in for an appointment. I keep them in my car because God knows the house is already bad enough, but I know they are not tasteful. I can't put them under the seat, because my car, like all the cars we've ever owned, has developed Car Leprosy, which causes all the nonessential parts such as window cranks to gradually fall off and collect under the seat and merge with French fries from the drive-thru window at the Burger King. I'm not about to put my teeth down *there*. So they sit in plain view, grinning at me as I drive and snickering at my lack of taste.

My wife and I are learning to accept all this. We realize that if the present trends continue, we will not be able to admit people into our house without blindfolds. I can live with that. What I worry about is that we will get in trouble with the bank or the government or something. One day there will be a violent pounding on the door, and we will be subjected to a surprise inspection by the Committee of Normal Grown-ups, headed by my wife's home economics teacher and my shop teacher. They'll take one look at our curtains, and they'll take away our house and cars and put us in a special institution where the inmates are roused at 4:30 A.M., chained together, and forced to install wallpaper all day. Nancy Reagan would be the warden.

Barbecuing Is the Pits

WHAT COULD BE MORE FUN than an outdoor barbecue? I can think of several things offhand, such as watching the secretary of state fall into a vat of untreated sewage. But that would probably cause us to go to war in Nicaragua or somewhere, so I guess we'll have to settle for a barbecue.

The barbecue was invented more than eighty million years ago by Cro-Magnon Man, who was the son of Stephanie Cro and Eric Magnon, a primitive but liberated couple. Cro-Magnon Man used to eat dinosaur meat raw, and it tasted awful, worse than yogurt. One day, while Cro-Magnon Man was eating, lightning set a nearby log on fire. Cro-Magnon Man was so surprised that he dropped his dinosaur meat onto the fire, where it ignited and gave off a disgusting odor that drove off all the insects, which in those days were the size of mature eggplants and extremely vicious. "This is terrific," said Cro-Magnon Man, only nobody understood him

4

because English hadn't been invented yet.

Burning dinosaurs quickly became a major form of insect control. At large Cro-Magnon lawn parties, the hosts would put whole brontosauruses on the fire, and they would sizzle into the night, keeping the insects away and giving off a stench that lingers to this very day at the northern end of the New Jersey Turnpike.

Eventually, of course, they used up all the dinosaurs, which led to the discovery that if you put cows and pigs on your fire, you could not only drive away insects but in a pinch you could also eat the cows and pigs. This led to the invention of hamburgers and hot dogs, which are cows and pigs that have been ground up in Chicago and formed into little portable units that can be easily thrown on a fire. Today people rarely put entire cows on fires except in Texas, where lifting animals is a major cultural activity, second only to wearing big hats.

To hold your outdoor barbecue, you'll need several dozen units of cow or pig and a portable grill, or hibachi. ("Hibachi" is a Japanese word meaning "extremely flimsy grills that break at the slightest touch but Americans buy them anyway.") You'll also need fuel. At one time, people used wood, but then the Consumer Product Safety Commission discovered that wood is flammable and banned it. So today you are required to use charcoal, a mineral that forms in torn paper bags in supermarkets. The problem, of course, is that charcoal, being a mineral, does not burn. Neither does charcoal lighter fluid. Firemen routinely use charcoal lighter fluid to extinguish major refinery fires. So what actually heats your barbecue food is matches, hundreds and hundreds of matches that you heap onto your charcoal until they form a blaze.

While you're waiting for your matches to get going,

5

you should prepare a tangy barbecue sauce.

TANGY BARBECUE SAUCE RECIPE

1 cup broached onions
2 liters vanilla abstract
½ pound neat's-foot oil
2 tablespoons butter or oregano
1 fresh poltroon, diced

To Prepare: With floured hands, on a floured surface, standing on a floured floor, and just generally surrounded by mounds and mounds of flour, combine the ingredients in a greased 5 5/8" by 16 3/8" pan, then pour the mixture carefully into an ungreased 4 3/8" by 18 7/8" pan and heat it until a 1 3/8" blister forms, when you stick your hand into it.

Now place your meat units on the grill. They should burst into flames immediately. Let them burn until they're cooked the way you like them:

• RARE (5-10 minutes): The outside is burnt and welded to the grill; the inside is pink and swirling with cow and pig disease germs.
• MEDIUM (5-10 minutes): The outside and part of the inside are burnt; many of the disease germs, particularly the elderly and pregnant ones, are dying slow, painful deaths.
• WELL DONE (5-10 minutes): Both the outside and the inside are completely burnt; almost all the disease germs are dead, and the few remaining ones are making elaborate plans for revenge.

When your meat is done, extinguish it with the barbecue sauce or charcoal lighter, detach it from the grill with a spatula or sharp chisel, and serve it with something that people can eat, such as Fritos or turkey sandwiches. You should eat quickly, because the insects will monitor you from a safe distance and attack the instant the smoke clears.

A Solution to Housework

ALMOST ALL HOUSEWORK is hard and dangerous, involving the insides of ovens and toilets and the cracks between bathroom tiles, where plague germs fester. The only housework that is easy and satisfying is the kind where you spray chemicals on wooden furniture and smear them around until the wood looks shiny. This is the kind of housework they show on television commercials: a professional actress, posing as the Cheerful Housewife (IQ 43), dances around her house, smearing and shining, smearing and shining, until before she knows it her housework is done and she is free to spend the rest of the afternoon reading the bust-development ads in *Cosmopolitan* magazine. She never cleans her toilets. When they get dirty, she just gets another house. Lord knows they pay her enough.

Most of us would rather smear and shine than actually clean anything. For example, our house has a semifinished basement, which means it looks too much like a finished room to store old tires in, but too much like a basement to actually live in. Our semifinished basement has a semibathroom, and one time, several years ago, a small woodland creature crept into the house in the middle of the night and died in the shower

7

stall. This is common behavior in the animal world: many animals, when in danger, are driven by instinct to seek refuge in shower stalls.

Since we hardly ever go down to our semifinished basement, we didn't discover the dead woodland creature until several weeks after it crept in, at which time it was getting fairly ripe. Now obviously, the correct thing to do was clean it up, but this is the hard kind of housework. So instead we stayed upstairs and went into an absolute frenzy of smearing and shining, until you could not walk into our living room without wearing sunglasses, for fear of being blinded by the glare off the woodwork. Eventually, we managed to block the woodland creature out of our minds.

Several months later, our friend Rob, who is a doctor, came to visit. He stayed in our semifinished basement, but we noticed that he came upstairs to take showers. One of the first things they teach you in medical school is never to take a shower with a dead woodland creature. We were so embarrassed that we went down and cleaned up the shower stall, with a shovel and acid. But I doubt we'd have done it if Rob hadn't been there.

Our behavior is not unique. People have been avoiding housework for millions of years. Primitive man would stay in one cave until the floor was littered with stegosaurus bones and the walls were covered with primitive drawings, which were drawn by primitive children when their parents went out to dinner, and then the family would move to a new cave, to avoid cleaning the old one. That's how primitive man eventually got to North America.

In North America, primitive man started running out of clean caves, and he realized that *somebody* was going to have to start doing housework. He thought about it

8

long and hard, and finally settled on primitive woman. But he needed an excuse to get himself out of doing the housework, so he invented civilization. Primitive woman would say: "How about staying in the cave and helping with the housework today?" And primitive man would say: "I can't, dear: I have to invent fire." Or: "I'd love to, dear, but I think it's more important that I devise some form of written language." And off he'd go, leaving the woman with the real work.

Over the years, men came up with thousands of excuses for not doing housework—wars, religion, pyramids, the United States Senate—until finally they hit on the ultimate excuse: business. They built thousands of offices and factories, and every day, all over the country, they'd get up, eat breakfast, and announce: "Well, I'm off to my office or factory now." Then they'd just *leave,* and they wouldn't return until the house was all cleaned up and dinner was ready.

But then men made a stupid mistake. They started to believe that "business" really *was* hard work, and they started talking about it when they came home. They'd come in the door looking exhausted, and they'd say things like "Boy, I sure had a tough meeting today."

You can imagine how a woman who had spent the day doing housework would react to this kind of statement. She'd say to herself: "Meeting? He had a tough *meeting?* I've been on my hands and knees all day cleaning toilets and scraping congealed spider eggs off the underside of the refrigerator, and he tells me he had a tough *meeting?*"

That was the beginning of the end. Women began to look into "business," and they discovered that all you do is go to an office and answer the phone and do various things with pieces of paper and have meetings. So women began going to work, and now nobody does

9

housework, other than smearing and shining, and before long there's going to be so much crud and bacteria under the nation's refrigerators that we're all going to get diseases and die.

The obvious and fair solution to this problem is to let men do the housework for, say, the next six thousand years, to even things up. The trouble is that men, over the years, have developed an inflated notion of the importance of everything they do, so that before long they would turn housework into just as much of a charade as business is now. They would hire secretaries and buy computers and fly off to housework conferences in Bermuda, but they'd never clean anything. So men are out.

But there is a solution; there is a way to get people to willingly do housework. I discovered this by watching household-cleaner commercials on television. What I discovered is that many people who seem otherwise normal will do virtually any idiot thing *if they think they will be featured in a commercial.* They figure if they get on a commercial, they'll make a lot of money, like the Cheerful Housewife, and they'll be able to buy cleaner houses. So they'll do *anything.*

For example, if I walked up to you in the middle of a supermarket and asked you to get down and scrub the floor with two different cleansers, just so I could see which one worked better, you would punch me in the mouth. But if I had guys with cameras and microphones with me, and I asked you to do the same thing, you'd probably do it. Not only that, but you'd make lots of serious, earnest comments about the cleansers. You'd say: "I frankly believe that New Miracle Swipe, with its combination of grease fighters and wax shiners, is a more effective cleanser, I honestly do. Really. I mean it."

You'd say this in the same solemn tone of voice you might use to discuss the question of whether the United States should deploy Cruise missiles in Western Europe. You'd have no shame at all.

So here's my plan: I'm going to get some old cameras and microphones and position them around my house. I figure that before long I'll have dozens of people just *dying* to do housework in front of my cameras. Sure, most of them will eventually figure out that they're not going to be in a commercial, but new ones will come along to replace them. Meanwhile, I'll be at work.

Three●Pronged Attack

I HAVE TWO MAJOR COMPLAINTS about electricity.

First, I cannot understand my electricity bills. I never even read them anymore: I just pay whatever random amount the electric company puts after "PAY THIS AMOUNT."

Frankly, I suspect the electric company doesn't have the vaguest notion how much electricity I use. I have an electric meter, but it is on the side of the house where a large contingent of killer wasps has lived since 1977, and *nobody,* not even my dog, ever goes there. I suspect that whoever is supposed to read my meter is lying out in the bushes somewhere, covered with stings.

So I think the electric company is just making my bill up out of thin air. Oh, they're very clever about it: They make the bill so elaborate that I won't suspect anything. It looks like this:

Adjusted basic flat usage charge rate: $34.70
Charge for usage of adjusted basic flat: $22.67

Flatly basic adjustable usage rate: $17.31
Maladjustment of usable, chargeable flat rate: $4.12
Ferrous Mineral Tax: $5.12
Tax to Pay Off the Spanish-American War Debt: $2.89
Gratuity: $1.68

As I said, I always pay these bills. I'm afraid that if I don't pay, the electric company will send huge jolts of electricity through the wire: one minute I'd be carving poultry with the electric carving knife, and the next minute I'd be a shriveled lump of carbon lying on the kitchen floor. So I pay, but I don't like it.

My other major electrical complaint concerns appliance plugs. You may have noticed that something very sinister has happened to appliance plugs since you were a child. I grew up during the Eisenhower administration in a normal, God-fearing home with a normal, God-fearing electrical system. All the outlets had two holes, and all the appliance plugs had two prongs, and everything worked just fine. Also the inflation rate was very low.

Now, suddenly, the appliance manufacturers are putting *three* prongs on their plugs, and *you can't plug them in*. What is going on? Has there been some huge mistake in the shipping department, so we're all getting appliances that were supposed to go to Yugoslavia? Has the government decided that appliances are so dangerous that consumers shouldn't be allowed to plug them in? Maybe it has something to do with the metric system. Whatever it is, it's a problem.

The simplest solution is to get a hacksaw and saw off the third prong. Unfortunately, this is a violation of federal law. It's like removing those little pillow tags that say "DO NOT REMOVE UNDER PENALTY OF

LAW." If you are convicted, agents of the Consumer Product Safety Commission will come to your house and lock you in a room filled with government safety publications and not let you out until you can pass an eight-hour written safety test.

So most people use those little plug adapters. This seems to work fine, but if you read the appliance instructions carefully, you'll note that plug adapters are Not Recommended:

WARNING: IF YOU USE ONE OF THOSE LITTLE PLUG ADAPTERS TO PLUG THIS APPLIANCE IN, ALL THE WARRANTIES AND GUARANTEES AND PROMISES THE SALES-MAN MADE ARE NULL AND VOID AND YOU MAY BE UNABLE TO HAVE CHILDREN.

The most radical solution to the three-pronged plug problem is to build a new house with three-hole outlets, or rewire your old house (which costs about the same). But this is really no solution at all, because as soon as everybody has three-hole outlets, the appliance manufacturers will come out with *four*-pronged plugs, and it will just keep escalating until your average plug contains so much metal that you will need the help of three or four strong men just to lift it.

So there is no good way you can solve the three-pronged plug problem. I think you should write your congressman and tell him to get off his butt and do something about it. Tell him you want the Defense Department to have a few large army tanks cruise up to the appliance manufacturers' factories and suggest that they start producing two-pronged plugs again pronto. And while you're at it, tell your congressman to straighten out the electric-bill mess, and maybe do something about my wasps.

13

They've Got Our Number

WHAT I LIKE BEST about the telephone is that it keeps you in touch with people, particularly people who want to sell you magazine subscriptions in the middle of the night. These people have been abducted by large publishing companies and placed in barbed-wire enclosures surrounded by armed men with attack dogs, and unless they sell 350 magazine subscriptions per day, they will not be fed. These people are desperate. They will say *anything* to get you to subscribe, and you cannot stop them merely by being rude:

CALLER: Hello, Mr. Barry?

ME: No, this is Adolf Hitler.

CALLER: Of course. My mistake. The reason I'm calling you at eleven-thirty at night, Mr. Hitler, is that I'm conducting a marketing survey, and—

ME: Are you selling magazine subscriptions?

CALLER: Magazine subscriptions? Me? Selling them? Ha ha. No. Certainly not. Not at all. No, this is just a plain old marketing survey. *(Sound of dogs barking in the background.)* If you'll just answer a few questions, we'll send you a million dollars.

ME: Well, what do you want to know?

CALLER: Well, I just want to ask you some questions about your household, such as how many people live there, and what their ages are, and what their incomes are, and whether any of them might be interested in subscribing to *Redbook?*

ME: I don't want to subscribe to anything, you lying piece of slime.

CALLER: How about *Time? Sports Illustrated?*

American Beet Farmer?

ME: I'm going to hang up.

CALLER: No! *(The dog,s get louder.)* Please! You can have my daughter!

ME: *(Click.)*

THE FIRST TELEPHONE was invented in 1876, when Alexander Graham Bell attached a battery to a crude electrical device and spoke into it. Everybody thought he was an idiot.

He would have died in poverty if Thomas Edison hadn't invented the second telephone several years later.

The first telephone systems were primitive "party lines," where everybody could hear what everybody else was talking about. This was very confusing:

BERTHA: Emma? I'm calling to tell you I seen your boy Norbert shootin' his musket at our goat again, and if you don't—

CLEM: This ain't Emma. This is Clem Johnson, and I got to reach Doc Henderson, because my wife Nell is all rigid and foaming at the mouth, and if she don't snap out of it soon the roast is going to burn.

EMMA: Norbert don't even own a musket. All he got is a bow and arrow, and he couldn't hit a steam locomotive from six feet, what with his bad hand, which he got when your boy Percy bit it, and which is festerin' pretty bad.

DOC HENDERSON: You better let me take a look at it.

BERTHA: The goat? Oh, he ain't hurt that bad, Doc. He's mostly just skittery on account of the musket fire.

15

CLEM: Now she's startin' to roll her eyes around. Looks like two hard-boiled eggs.

EMMA: What kind of roast is it?

DOC HENDERSON: If it's just skittery, you should stroke it a bit and keep it in a dark place.

EMMA: Well, I ain't no doctor, but I ain't never heard of stroking a roast.

CLEM: Only dark place we got is the barn, and I'd be afraid to put Nell in there on account of she'd scare the chickens.

BERTHA: Chickens ain't a *roast,* Clem; chickens is *poultry.* Take 'em out of the oven when you can wiggle the drumstick.

EMMA: I tole you already, Norbert don't even own a musket.

CALLER: Hi. I'm conducting a marketing survey. Is Mr. Hitler at home?

CLEM: No, but I'll take a year's worth of *American Beet Farmer* if you got it.

THE PARTY-LINE SYSTEM led to a lot of unnecessary confusion and death, so the phone company devised a system whereby you can talk to only one person at a time, although not necessarily the person you want. In fact, if you call any large company, you will *never* get to talk to the person you're calling. Large companies employ people who are paid, on a commission basis, solely to put calls on hold. The only exception is department stores, where all calls are immediately routed to whichever clerk has the most people waiting in line for service.

But we should never complain about our telephone system. It is the most sophisticated system in the world, yet it is the easiest to use. For example, my twenty-

16

month-old son, who cannot perform a simple act like eating a banana without getting much of it in his hair, is perfectly capable of direct-dialing Okinawa, and probably already has. In another year, he'll be able to order his own magazine subscriptions.

Okay, Now Try the Engine

YOU SHOULD DO YOUR OWN CAR REPAIRS. It's an easy way to save money and possibly maim yourself for life.

You're probably afraid to repair your car because you think cars are complicated. This is nonsense. Many teenage boys understand cars, and on any scale of intellectual achievement teenage boys rank right down there with newts. At least they did when I was one of them.

When I was in high school, we boys would stand out on the corner at lunchtime and smoke unfiltered cigarettes and spit frequently, and guys would pull up in genuinely hideous-looking cars with the front ends jacked way up. They'd open the hoods and we'd stare inside and have conversations like this:

LOOKERS: Three eighty-nine?
DRIVER: Four twenty-seven.
LOOKERS: Fuel-injected?
DRIVER: Headers.
LOOKERS: Dual?
DRIVER: Quad.
LOOKERS: Boss.

Then we'd all spit approvingly. Sometimes the conversation would turn ugly, particularly if some

17

participants favored Fords and some favored Chevrolets. The Ford-Chevrolet conflict was a major issue, considerably more important to us than, say, the fate of the Free World. Those who favored Fords would yell "Fo Mo Co," which is short for "Ford Motor Company." Those who favored Chevrolets would yell "Fo No Go," which is short for "Ford No Go." This was considered a very witty insult. Sometimes fights would break out.

What I'm getting at is that we had the intellectual depth of lima beans, and *we still managed to understand cars.* So you can, too.

The trouble with most do-it-yourself car articles is they tell you how to do things you don't really need to do, like change the oil. Most such articles rave on for *pages* about changing the oil, as if it were some kind of sacred ritual, never once telling you how degrading and pointless it is. I have been driving for eighteen years, and I have never once had a car problem I could have solved by changing the oil. If the Good Lord had wanted us to change the oil, He would have put different oil in the car in the first place.

But if you believe the do-it-yourself articles, you traipse along, changing your oil regularly, and one day your car ceases to run, and you try changing the oil a couple more times, and it *still* doesn't run, and you end up taking it to an auto mechanic, and you have this conversation:

YOU: What's wrong?

MECHANIC: It seems to be either the transmission or the engine. *(Translation: "I'm not sure, so I plan to replace every part in the car.")*

YOU: How long will it take to fix?

MECHANIC: We should have a pretty good idea by

Friday. *("One hundred and sixty-two years.")*

YOU: How much will it cost?

MECHANIC: Well, I have to check on some of the parts and labor, but figure about $130. *("Eight billion skillion dollars.")*

So what you need to know is how to do *major* car repairs, the kind most do-it-yourself articles don't talk about. There are two major kinds of car problems, which we in the automotive community refer to as the Two Major Kinds of Car Problems:

• *Problems that cause your car to make loud noises.*

What you do here is *turn up the radio.* If your car doesn't have a radio, you can sing loudly as you drive. Some people try to deal with noise problems by messing around with the muffler, but I advise against this. Mufflers are filthy, disgusting objects covered with parts of every dead animal you have ever run over. I would no more touch a muffler than I would change my oil.

• *Problems that cause your car to stop.*

Generally these problems involve the engine, which is a large object you'll find under your hood, unless you live in a high-crime area. Open the hood and poke around among the wires with a screwdriver, or, if you have no screwdriver, the tip of an umbrella. Have somebody sit in the car. As you poke, yell "Try it now" or "Okay, try it now." This is how most professional mechanics solve engine problems. Before long you'll be fixing cars as well as they do, by which I mean about 30 percent of the time.

The Problem with Pets

EVERYBODY SHOULD HAVE A PET. Pets give you all the love and devotion of close relatives, but you can lock them in the basement for hours at a time if they get loud or boring. The pets, I mean.

Have you ever wondered why people have pets? Neither have I. I suspect it's because pets are easy to talk to. I spend hours talking to my dog, explaining my views on world affairs. She always listens very attentively, although I'm not sure she understands me. If I could hear what she's thinking, it would probably go like this:

ME: The situation in the Middle East certainly looks serious.

MY DOG: I wonder if he's going to give me some food.

ME: It is unfortunate that an area so vital to the economic well-being of the world is so politically unstable.

MY DOG: Maybe he'll give me some food now.

ME: The Russians certainly are making it difficult for our government to achieve a lasting Mideast peace.

MY DOG: Any minute now he might go into the kitchen and get me some food.

My first pet was a group of ants in one of those educational ant farms with clear plastic sides. My mother gave it to me for Christmas when I was about ten. She had to send away to Chicago to buy the ants. The ironic thing is that our house was already overrun with local ants, which came out during the summer in hordes. I mean, it was like one of those science fiction movies in which insects take over the Earth. Every summer we had huge, brazen ants striding around the kitchen demanding food and running up long distance telephone charges. My mother spent much of her time whapping at them with brooms and spraying them with deadly chemicals. Nothing worked. The ants used to lie on their backs, laughing at the brooms and the chemicals and calling for more.

What I'm getting at is that my mother hated ants, but she sent good money all the way to Chicago so I could have ants for Christmas. Christmas does horrible things to people's values.

Anyway, I got the ants and put them into their ant farm and fed them sugar and water. The idea was that they would build a lot of ant tunnels and stuff and I would learn about Nature. Instead, they died. My mother was astounded. I mean, here she spends whole summers trying to kill local ants that she got for free, and these Chicago ants, ants that she paid money for, ants that had their own little farm and their own little food, just die. If we had been smart, we would have put our local ants into the ant farm and fed them sugar and water; that probably would have polished them off.

The lesson to be learned here is that insects make lousy pets. Even the best-trained, most intelligent, and most loyal insect pets tend to look and behave very much like ordinary common-criminal insects. Also you can't explain your views on world affairs to an insect, unless you drink a lot.

FISH AND GREEN CHEESE

Tropical fish are not much better. My wife and I went through a fish period, during which we spent hundreds of thousands of dollars on tanks and pumps

21

and filters and chemicals and special plants and special rocks and special food. We had enough tropical fish technology to land a tropical fish on the moon. What we could not do was keep any given tropical fish alive for longer than a week. Just as soon as we'd pop one in the tank, it would develop Fin Rot. Medical science has developed no cure for Fin Rot, so our fish would languish around among the fish technology, rotting. We were constantly buying replacement fish. Whenever one of us would leave the house, the other would say: "Don't forget to pick up several tropical fish." I have no actual proof, but I strongly suspect that these fish were manufactured in Chicago.

The most popular pets are dogs and cats. Now when I say "dogs," I'm talking about dogs, which are large, bounding, salivating animals, usually with bad breath. I am not talking about those little squeaky things you can hold on your lap and carry around. Zoologically speaking, these are not dogs at all; they are members of the pillow family.

Anyway, dogs make good pets because they are very loyal. (NOTE: When I say "loyal," I mean "stupid." I once wrote a column in which I said dogs are stupid, and I got a lot of nasty mail from people who insisted, often with misspelled words, that dogs are intelligent. Perhaps from their point of view dogs are intelligent, but I don't want to get into that here. I'll just stick with "loyal.")

Yes indeed, dogs are loyal. Here is an example of how loyal dogs are: When two dogs meet, they will spend the better part of a day sniffing each other's private parts and going to the bathroom on any object more than one inch high. Talk about loyalty.

Cats are less loyal than dogs, but more independent. (This is code. It means: "Cats are smarter than dogs, but they hate people.") Many people love cats. From time to time, newspapers print stories about some elderly widow who died and left her entire estate, valued at $320,000, to her cat, Fluffkins. Cats read these stories, too, and are always plotting to get named as beneficiaries in their owners' wills. Did you ever wonder where your cat goes when it wanders off for several hours? It meets with other cats in estate-planning seminars. I just thought you should know.

Governmental Follies

Fungus on the Economy

I DON'T KNOW ABOUT YOU, but I was ever so grateful when President Reagan and several other top leaders got together a few years back and straightened out the world economy. I had been meaning to do something about it myself, but I never found the time on account of we've had a lot of rain lately, which has caused these fungal growths to sprout all over the lawn.

I am not talking here about toadstools. I am talking about organisms reminiscent of the one that nearly ate the diner in the Ingmar Bergman film *The Blob* before Steve McQueen subdued it with a fire extinguisher. Of course Steve had to deal with just the one lone, isolated growth, whereas I have several dozen, and I couldn't possibly extinguish them all if they attacked in unison. Eventually they're going to figure this out. I mean, they may be fungal growths, but they're not stupid.

Anyway, with all this on my mind I've had very little time to spend on the world economy, which is why I was so glad to hear that the leaders of the economic bloc known to economists as the Big Rich Western Nations with Indoor Plumbing and Places That Sell Cheeseburgers met in Williamsburg to straighten things out. Williamsburg is an authentic colonial restored place in Virginia where people in authentic uncomfortable clothing demonstrate how horrible it was to live in historical colonial times. Back then, if you wanted one crummy bar of soap, you had to spend the better part of a week melting beeswax and rendering pigs and all the other degrading things people did before the invention of the supermarket. This is how people still live in a lot of wretched little Third World nations with names like Koala Paroondi, whose leaders were not invited to Williamsburg because the Western leaders were afraid they'd eat all the food.

The economic summit cost something like eight million dollars, which sounds like a lot of money until you realize it lasted almost four days. The reason it took the leaders so long to straighten out the world economy is that they had to wrestle with some very complex issues. For example, I read in *Newsweek* that French President Mitterrand does not like white sauces, and West German Chancellor Kohl does not like seafood, and so on. These high-level food differences often resulted in Frank Exchanges of Views during the summit meals:

FRENCH PRESIDENT MITTERRAND: Please pass the tiny lobsters dish.

BRITISH PRIME MINISTER THATCHER: Those are not "tiny lobsters." Those are crayfish.

MITTERRAND: Fish? Do not make me laugh. I represent the greatest food snots in the world, and I know what is the fish and what is not the fish, and this is not the fish. Regard: it has the claws. Does this fish of the cray have the claws?

THATCHER: Yes, you twit. It's a crustacean.

MITTERRAND: Perhaps I am a twit, but at least I am not wearing the tweedy British clothings of such monumental dowdiness that a dog would be reluctant to relieve itself upon them.

ANOTHER PROBLEM WAS INTEREST RATES. Interest rates are very high, and the leaders spent a lot of time during their high-level meals trying to come up with a solution.

Finally—and this just goes to show you why these people are world leaders and you are a mere taxpayer—they decided that *interest rates ought to come down*. It's a radical plan, but it just might work.

From the United States' point of view, the big issue at Williamsburg was unfair foreign competition, which means any competition that involves foreigners. At one time, the foreigners competed fairly: they made chocolates and little carved-wood figurines, and we made everything else. Then, without warning, foreigners began making reasonably priced, well-made, technologically advanced cars, television sets, shoes, mushrooms, et cetera, and they forced Americans to buy these things at gunpoint. President Reagan discussed this problem at Williamsburg with Japanese Prime Minister Nakasone, and they hammered out an agreement under which the Japanese will continue to send us cars, but they'll start putting defects in them. We're going to give them technical assistance: we're going to send people over there to train Japanese factory workers to be hostile and alienated and put the transmission in wrong and stuff like that.

At the end of the summit, the leaders issued a major economic-policy statement that nobody read except the editors of the *New York Times* and everybody went home. The world economy began to improve almost immediately. Even as you read these words, the yen is rising vs. the franc. Or else it's falling. You may rest assured that the yen is doing whatever it does vs. the franc when things are improving. Also the other day my son ran his tricycle over one of the growths, and the growth let him off with only a sharp reprimand. So things are really looking up.

Give Wall Street Credit

I THINK I'LL JUST QUICKLY bring us all up to date on President Reagan's plan to save the economy, so we can get back to whatever we were doing.

The big problem is Wall Street, which is a street in New York City where people go every day to work themselves into a lather. To understand how Wall Street works, all you have to do is recall those television commercials for a major Wall Street brokerage firm, the ones that feature cattle. It is not mere chance that the firm chose cattle as its symbol. If you spend much time with cattle, you know they spend their time making cattle mess and panicking. The scene is pretty much the same on Wall Street, except the herd members carry briefcases. They are very skittery, and for good reason: they are in the world's silliest business. Here's how it works:

Say a company wants some money. It prints up a batch of pieces of paper ("stocks"), goes down to Wall Street, and looks around for some herd members to sell the paper to. "Hey there," the company says to the herd members. "How would you like to own a piece of paper? Look at these features: It has an attractive border, three different colors of ink, and many financial words such as 'accrual' and 'debenture' printed right on it." The herd members snuffle around for a while, then one of them bolts up and buys a piece of paper. Then, suddenly, they're trampling all over each other to buy pieces of paper.

The company now has a large sum of money, and it departs hurriedly, chuckling, to buy factories or executive washrooms or whatever. Gradually, the herd members realize that all *they* have is paper, which is utterly worthless unless they can get other herd members to buy it. So they all end up simply trading paper back and forth, day after day, year after year. Deep in their souls, they realize they are participating in an enormous hoax that could collapse at any moment, so any event, no matter how trivial, causes them to panic. You can pick up the newspaper financial section any day and read stories like this:

NEW YORK—Stock prices plunged sharply today as investors reacted to the discovery that Saturn actually has six moons, rather than five as was believed previously.

So the stock market is always skittering up and down. When Ronald Reagan was elected, it skittered up for a while, because Ron promised he would reduce government spending. Wall Street fears the government because the government is Wall Street's major competitor in the worthless-pieces-of-paper business.

But it turned out that what Ron really meant was he was going to reduce one *kind* of government spending, so he could spend more money on the MX Missile, the B-1 Bomber, the Cruise Missile, the Atomic Dirigible, the Secret Decoder Ring, and the Deadly Outer Space Death Ray. So he ended up with a budget that actually *increases* government spending, for the 206th year in a row.

Once Wall Street realized what Ron had done, it worked itself into an even bigger panic than usual. Ron has been trying to calm it down, but the herd members are too busy barging around, wild-eyed, waving their pieces of paper. Ron may have to go to Wall Street personally and deliver a soothing speech. "There, there," he would tell the herd. "There, there."

Ron's other big problem is the Federal Reserve Board. Nobody knows much about the Federal Reserve Board: it is a secret society whose members periodically emerge from their mountain hideout, raise the interest rates, then scurry off into the darkness. This forces the banks to raise the prime rate, which is the rate they charge customers who do not want or need money.

One result of all this interest-rate raising is that financial institutions have cooked up all kinds of bizarre schemes to get you to give them money. You can't pick up a newspaper or turn on the television these days without seeing advertisements for these schemes:

"Attention savers: If you invest in our new All Savers Money Market Fund Treasury Bond Certificates of Deposit, you can earn 23.6 percent interest, which, compounded hourly and during neap tides, will yield an actualized semiannual net deductible pretax liquid return of 41.7 percent, although of course your mileage may vary. If you are found guilty of premature withdrawal, the federal government requires us to send people around to break your legs, so be sure to thumb through the prospectus."

I have a lot of trouble understanding these schemes, so for the time being I am investing my money in groceries and consumer objects that I can charge on my Sears credit card.

Outbungling the Commies

LET'S ALL WRITE our congresspersons and demand that the United States become involved in a no-win military quagmire in Central America.

The reason? Global strategy. To understand the strategic significance of Central America, let's take a close look at the map, especially in the critical region where the Oswego River flows into Lake Ontario. No, wait. Wrong map.

Ah, Here we are. Look closely at Central America, and try to imagine what would happen if this vital region were to fall into Communist hands. What would happen is a lot of Communists would be stung repeatedly by vicious tropical insects the size of mature hamsters.

We cannot afford to have this happen. We cannot afford to have a horde of Communists down there becoming so cranky and welt-covered that eventually, just for an excuse to get out of the jungle, they foment a revolution in Mexico, which means you'd have Communist guerrilla troops right next to Texas. I doubt they could take Texas by force. Texas has the largest fleet of armed pickup trucks of any major power, and any invading guerrilla army would be shot and run over repeatedly before it got half a mile, especially if it invaded on a Saturday night.

So the Communists would have to use a psychological approach. They'd win the Texans over by such ploys as holding barbecues, wearing big hats and promising to extend the football season. Once Texas went Communist, Oklahoma would follow quickly, followed by Nebraska, followed by whatever state is next to Nebraska, and so on until the entire nation had turned Communist except Massachusetts, which is already very left-wing and consequently would turn Republican.

It is to prevent this kind of tragedy that we're sending bales of your tax money to buy guns for the corrupt, murderous slime buckets who run El Salvador. And for those of you weak-willed, sob-sister, namby-pamby probable homosexuals who think this is wrong, let me point out that if we don't prop up our slime buckets, the Communists will install *their* corrupt slime buckets, and you can bet your bottom tax dollar that the peasants down there are much happier being oppressed by ours. "Anything to keep Texas safe" is the traditional El Salvadoran peasant motto.

Besides, the El Salvadoran rulers have started showing a real interest in human rights since we put them on this clever incentive plan under which we threaten to stop sending them guns if they keep using them to shoot their own citizens. This plan is working very well: Reagan administration observers have keen bringing back rave reviews. "They're not killing nearly as many innocent women and children," the observers report, beaming with pride. "Let's send them some more guns."

But guns alone are not enough, which is why Texas does not control the world. You also need troops, and the Communists are sending Cuban troops to Central America. Truth to tell, you can't wave your arms in a world trouble spot without striking Cuban troops. They'll go anywhere, because if they stay home they have to listen to extremely long speeches.

I say that if the Communists are sending troops, they must have a damned good reason, and we should send troops, too. Only I don't think we should send our armed forces, because I have serious reservations about how they'd do in an actual war. I suspect most of them enlisted because of those really slick, upbeat TV commercials suggesting that all you do in the armed forces is grin and jog and learn meaningful career skills such as tank repair. If we sent these kids to Central America, they'd go jogging into the jungle, grinning and clutching their tank-repair tools, and the only question would be whether the Communists would get them before the insects did.

So I say we send the people who really understand the Communist threat in Central America, the very people who alerted us to it in the first place. I'm talking about the Reagan administration's foreign policy strategists. I say we arm them to the teeth with insect repellent, fly them over the jungle and drop them at night. We could even give them parachutes.

It's Drafty in Here

IF YOU CAN possibly manage it, you should avoid being a young person or a wheat farmer when the president starts feeling international tension. Nine times out of ten, when a president gets mad at the Russians, he does something nasty to young people or wheat farmers, and sometimes both.

For example, when the Russians invaded Afghanistan, President Jimmy Carter was so angry that he ordered teenage American males to register for the draft; told the U.S. Olympic team it couldn't go to the Olympics; and told farmers they couldn't sell wheat to Russia. If you didn't know any better, you'd have thought Afghanistan had been invaded by teenage American wheat farmers, led by the U.S. Olympic team. I imagine that if Jimmy had been *really* angry at the Russians, he would have had the Olympic team lined up and shot.

But eventually everybody got bored with Afghanistan. The Russians remained there; the farmers went back to selling them wheat; and the Olympic athletes found occupations that were less directly connected with international tension than, say, the parallel bars. Jimmy went on to other pursuits, such as losing the election. But draft registration continued.

When Ronald Reagan was campaigning for president, he said he was dead set against peacetime registration, on the grounds that in a free country the government shouldn't go around forcing people to do things. It turns out he was just kidding. He recently decided to continue registration, using the same logic that Jimmy did: although at the moment we are not technically in a war with the Russians, we could get into one any day, and if we do, we could have our Army up to snuff six weeks faster if we have the teenagers already registered. I see only one minor flaw in this reasoning, which is that if we ever *do* get into a war with the Russians, we will probably be melted, teenagers and all, in the first half hour or so, which would tend to disrupt the training process.

Aside from that flaw, I think registration is a terrific idea. When the national security is at stake, I think everybody should be obligated to register, regardless of age, sex, religion, or occupation. The only exceptions should be children, women, and anybody else who is not a teenage male.

Perhaps you're wondering why we single out teenage males. Some people believe it's because teenagers are the most physically fit, but that is stupid. If physical fitness were the main reason, we would register professional athletes first. The truth is that we register teenage males because:

- We always have.
- Many teenage males are sullen and snotty and could use a little discipline.
- There are fewer of them than there are of us.
- If we tried to register older people, they would write

letters to their congressmen and hire sharp lawyers, and we'd never be able to get anybody into the Army.

So when we draft people, we always start with teenage males. This means that the President, his advisers, and the members of Congress usually don't get a chance to serve, but that is one of the burdens of public office.

Many Army officials would like to start drafting teenagers right away, but unfortunately they don't have any actual war going on at the moment, so they're stuck with trying to get people to volunteer. This is very difficult, because the Army is not generally perceived as being a fun organization. Most people think that the Army is a place where you get up early in the morning to be yelled at by people with short haircuts and tiny brains.

The Army has been trying very hard to change its image. It has produced a bunch of television commercials suggesting that it is really just a large technical school, where everybody is happy and nobody ever gets sent to wretched foreign countries to get shot at. I think these commercials are on the right track but don't go far enough. I think they should make the Army look more as it does on "M*A*S*H," where the characters have so much fun that most of them have remained in the Army for ten years:

HAWKEYE: Boy, war sure is awful, isn't it? Ha ha.

BJ: Ha ha, it sure is. Say, I have an idea: Let's go drink a bunch of martinis and flirt with attractive nurses and play practical jokes on various stuffed shirts, as we have every night since this series began.

HAWKEYE: Ha ha. Good idea, BJ. But first let's fix

these wounded soldiers, who are a constant reminder that war is an enormous waste of human life, although fortunately the major characters never get killed.

BJ: Ha ha.

IF THE ARMY commercials were more like "M*A*S*H," I think lots of teenagers would want to enlist. In fact, I think just about everybody would want to enlist, for a chance to pal around with Alan Alda. The Army would have all the people it would need, and everything would be swell—unless, of course, we got into an actual war. Then we'd have to turn things over to the teenage males.

MX Is the Way to Go. 'Bye

I REALIZE IT'S NONE OF MY BUSINESS, but I have a few questions about the MX missile system. Here, as I understand it, is how the MX is supposed to work: We would put a bunch of missiles where the Russians can't hit them with their missiles. That way, if the Russians shoot at us, we'll be able to shoot back, and everybody will wind up dead. This is considered to be much more desirable than what would happen without the MX, namely that the Russians would still be alive and we would be dead. Obviously, the best solution would be for us to be alive and the Russians to be dead, but for this to happen we would have to shoot first, and we wouldn't do that because the whole reason we built all these nuclear devices in the first place is to preserve world peace. So we are going for the peace-loving solution, which is to guarantee that if anybody attacks anybody, everybody winds up dead.

So far so good. I mean, any fool can see the MX is the way to go. But what troubles me is the particular *kind* of MX President Reagan decided to build. Basically, the people who worry about our national defense for us came up with two options:

OPTION ONE: Dig several thousand holes in Nevada and Utah, but put actual missiles in only a few of them, so the Russians won't know which holes to shoot at.

Cost: A trillion or so dollars.

Advantages: The bulldozer industry would prosper beyond its wildest dreams.

Disadvantages: It won't work. One flaw, of course, is that the Russians, using their spy satellites, could figure out which holes we put the missiles in. We could probably come up with some crafty scheme to overcome this flaw: Maybe we'd attach leaves and fruit to the missiles, so the Russians would think we were merely planting enormous trees in Nevada and Utah; or maybe we'd put huge signs on each missile with the words "THIS IS NOT A MISSILE" printed in Russian. So hiding the missiles is not the problem. The problem is that the Russians, if they have any sense at all, would simply build more missiles and shoot at *all* the holes, and we'd all wind up dead with no way to make the Russians dead. So the national defense people came up with Option Two.

OPTION TWO: Put the MX missiles in holes we already have.

Cost: A few hundred billion dollars.

Advantages: None, except it costs less, which is not really an advantage because the government will spend the leftover money on some other gigantic scheme anyway.

Disadvantages: It won't work, since the Russians

already know where the existing holes are. Heck, *I* even know where they are. They're in Kansas. All the Russians would have to do is locate a map revealing the location of Kansas, which they could probably do, what with their extensive spy network.

SO BASICALLY, President Reagan was faced with two options, both of which involved holes and neither of which would work. He pondered this problem for a while, on his horse, and finally decided to go with Option Two. Why, he reasoned, should we pay a trillion dollars for a system that wouldn't work, when we can get the same thing for a few hundred billion? He's going on the time-honored axiom that if something is not worth doing, it is not worth doing right.

Ideally, President Reagan would have delayed his decision in the hope that, given time, his defense planners could have come up with a third option, such as covering Nebraska with ice and launching the missiles from dogsleds. But he had to act fast, because of the Window of Vulnerability. The Window of Vulnerability, which was discovered only recently, is the period of time between now and whenever we finish the MX system, during which we are vulnerable to Russian attack. Reagan's defense advisers are very big on the Window of Vulnerability: for months now, they have been running around the country proclaiming how *vulnerable* we are. This puzzles me. I mean, if we're so vulnerable, why are we telling everybody? And if the Russians are so hot to attack us, why don't they do it now? Why on earth would they wait until after we finish our MX system? And if they don't attack us when we're vulnerable, why do we need the MX at all? These questions deserve a lot of hard thought, which I intend to give them just as soon as I've had another drink.

MX Service Warranty

I'M A LITTLE worried about the MX missile system. Don't get me wrong: I certainly think we *need* another missile system. Better safe than sorry, that's my motto.

What I'm worried about is that we won't be able to get anybody to *repair* the MX. You can't get *anything* repaired these days. Take, for example, *Voyager 2,* a United States space rocket that recently flew to Saturn to take pictures. It worked okay for a while, but then the camera got pointed in the wrong direction and started sending back pictures of outer space. This was bad public relations: taxpayers don't want to pay nine zillion dollars for pictures that look like the inside of somebody's closet with the light off. The NASA scientists claim *Voyager* 2 is a success anyway, but they have to claim this, because otherwise they can't ask for more money. They would have claimed *Voyager* 2 was a success even if it had crashed into Phoenix, Arizona. The truth is, *Voyager* 2 broke and they couldn't get it repaired.

This is a problem not only with rockets, but with other major appliances as well. If you have ever called the service department of a major department store to get an appliance repaired, you know what I am talking about:

YOU: Hello, my washer—
TAPE RECORDING: Thank you for calling the

Service Department. All of our service representatives are smoking cigarettes and chatting; your call will be taken just as soon as somebody feels like taking your call. Thank you.

(For the next thirty-five minutes, you listen to a medley of songs by Barry Manilow, who has written a great many songs. Perhaps too many. Then an actual service representative comes on the line.)

SERVICE REPRESENTATIVE: Thank you for calling the Service Department. How may we serve you?

YOU: It's our washer. One of the drive belts snared my wife by the arm and she can't get loose and we can't turn it off and we're worried about what will happen when it gets to the spin cycle.

SERVICE REPRESENTATIVE: When did you purchase the washer?

YOU: A year ago, I guess. Could you hurry please? It's almost done with the rinse cycle.

SERVICE REPRESENTATIVE: Then I'm afraid you are not covered under the ninety-day warranty. But don't feel bad: nobody is *ever* covered under the ninety-day warranty. That's why we offer it. Did you buy a maintenance agreement?

YOU: I don't *know,* for God's sake. *(Your wife screams in the background.)* Please, just get someone out here.

SERVICE REPRESENTATIVE: We will have a serviceperson in your area in a year or so. Will someone be at home?

YOU: I imagine my wife will. What's left of her.

SERVICE REPRESENTATIVE: Fine. We will have someone call you during the latter half of next year to let you know exactly what month the serviceperson will

42

be there. Thank you for calling the Service Department.

A FEW YEARS AGO, we had a serviceperson come to our house regularly to try to repair our television set. He had this ritual: He would arrive with six hundred pounds of tools, select a screwdriver, take the back off the television, and stare at the insides as if he had been raised by a primitive Brazilian jungle tribe and had never seen a television before. Then he would put the cover back on, load his six hundred pounds of tools back onto the truck, and leave. Once, to prove he was sincerely interested in the problem, he took the television with him and kept it for several months. Finally, my wife and I took the cover off ourselves and blew on the insides of the television; it worked fine after that, and the serviceperson didn't come around anymore, which was sort of a shame, because he was getting to be like one of the family.

Another time, the motor on our forty-five-dollar vacuum cleaner broke, so I took the vacuum to a serviceperson, who took it apart but couldn't fix the motor. So I sent it to the factory, which fixed the motor for twenty-five dollars but didn't put the vacuum cleaner together again. So finally I took the parts to the Service Center, which is where people go when they are really desperate. You go in and take a number, then you sit with the other appliance owners, who are clutching their toasters and radios and hoping the counter person will call their numbers before their food and water runs out.

Finally the counter person called my number, and I explained to him that my vacuum cleaner was not broken, that I merely wanted him to put it together again. I had trouble getting this message across, because the counter person had obviously spent several years in an IQ-reduction program. He'd say: "Well, what's wrong with it?" And I'd say: "*Nothing's* wrong with it. I just want you to put it together." And he'd say: "Well, what's wrong with it?" And so on.

Eventually, he got the picture, and he took my vacuum cleaner parts to the fellows back in the Shop, and together they came up with an estimate of $87 to put them together again. This means that we would have paid a total of $112 to repair a $45 cleaner, so instead we bought a new vacuum cleaner, which is, of course, what they wanted us to do in the first place.

WELL, I'M AFRAID the government will have the same sort of problem. They'll buy a snappy new MX missile system, and everything will be fine until the Russians attack us, at which point we'll have bombs raining down on Ohio while the guys down the Pentagon are sitting in the War Room, listening to Barry Manilow on the telephone. Think about it.

Birthday Celebration

THE NAME "FEBRUARY" comes from the Latin word *Februarius*, which means "fairly boring stretch of time during which one expects the professional ice hockey season to come to an end but it does not." During February we observe four special days, none of which is an excuse for serious drinking:

GROUNDHOG DAY, FEBRUARY 2
This is an old American tradition started years ago by profoundly retarded old Americans. According to the tradition, on this day Mr. Groundhog comes out of his

44

hole and looks around for media representatives, who make a major fuss about it. It is one of those things that only media people care about. Another one is the government of Canada.

LINCOLN'S BIRTHDAY, FEBRUARY 12

Abraham Lincoln grew up in the Tennessee wilderness and killed a bear when he was only three years old. No, wait: that was Davy Crockett. Abraham Lincoln grew up in a log cabin and read by candlelight and learned to spell by writing on the back of a coal shovel. Later on he wrote the Gettysburg Address on the back of an envelope. He had a pathological fear of normal paper. As a youth, Lincoln was famous for splitting rails. People were afraid to leave their rails lying around because Lincoln would sneak up and split them.

Lincoln became nationally known when he won the famous Lincoln-Douglas debates, sponsored by the League of Women Voters. Here is a complete transcript:

DOUGLAS: I think the territories should decide the slavery question for themselves, and I'm five feet seven inches tall.

LINCOLN: I disagree, and I'm six four.

After the debates, Lincoln became president and grew a beard because some little girl wrote him a letter and suggested it. He was crazy that way. We should all be grateful she didn't suggest he wear rouge.

ST. VALENTINE'S DAY, FEBRUARY 14

The *Encyclopaedia Britannica* says, "St. Valentine's Day as a lovers' festival and the modern tradition of sending valentine cards have no relation to the saints, but, rather, seem to be connected either with the Roman fertility festival of the Lupercalia or with the mating season of

45

birds."

This means that, at this very moment, your kids may be in school cutting out little construction-paper hearts to celebrate the sexual activity of Romans or birds. No wonder people don't go to church anymore.

WASHINGTON'S BIRTHDAY, FEBRUARY 16

Actually, George Washington was born on February 22. The government has decided that we should celebrate his birthday on the third Monday, because that way the nation gets a long weekend, and, what the hell, Washington is dead anyway. (When I say "the nation," of course, I mean "government employees and maybe six or seven other people.") I think that if the government can mess around with the calendar for its own convenience, the rest of us should be able to do the same thing. For example, most people find April 15 to be a terribly inconvenient day to file income tax returns, coming as it does right at the beginning of baseball season. I think this year on April 15 we should all send the government little notices explaining that we observe Income Tax Day on December 11.

But back to Washington. As a youth, he threw a cherry tree across the Delaware. Later he got wooden teeth and was chosen to represent Virginia at the Continental Congress, a group of colonists who wanted to revolt against the King because he made them wear wigs and tights. They chose Washington to lead their army because he was strong and brave and not in the room at the time. Everybody thought he would lose, but he outfoxed the British by establishing headquarters all over the place. Here on the East Coast you can't swing your arms without hitting one of Washington's headquarters. Finally the British, who

46

were Germans anyway, gave up and went home to fight the French, who were more conveniently located, and Washington became the Father of Our Country. That is why each year on a Monday somewhere around his birthday we have major-appliance sales oriented toward government employees.

Why Not a Postal Service?

EDITOR'S NOTE: This column appears at first to be about the Postal Service but may actually be about the neutron bomb. It's hard to tell.

I am all for the nine-digit Zip Code and the 37-cent stamp. In fact, I think the Postal Service ought to go even further: let's have a fifteen-digit Zip Code and a $4.50 stamp. Let's make it virtually impossible to send mail. I hate getting mail anyway. Apparently, my name is on a computerized mailing list entitled "People with Extremely Small Brains," and as a result I get mainly two kinds of mail:

• *Announcements Announcing Contests Somebody Else Will win:* "Mr. Barry, we are pleased to announce that you have been chosen as a semifinalist in the Publishers' Publishing House Sweepstakes, and may have already won 11,000 head of cattle and a Korean servant family."

• *Investment Opportunities for Morons:* "This rare opportunity to purchase a finely crafted, individually registered investment collection of Early American Colonial Jellied Candies is being

47

made available only to residents of North and South America, and will not be repeated unless people actually take us up on it."

I have learned to recognize this kind of mail from the envelopes, which always have gimmicky statements designed to arouse my curiosity ("If you do not open this envelope immediately, you will never see your children again"). So I usually throw the envelopes away without opening them. But this doesn't work: the junk mail companies have armies of workers who comb through everybody's garbage at night, retrieve their announcements, and put them right back in the mail.

We could solve this problem if we all bought portable blowtorches. We could stroll up to our mailboxes, open the doors, and incinerate everything inside. Or, for a more efficient approach, the Postal Service could buy larger blowtorches and incinerate everybody's mail right at the post offices. Ideally, the Postal Service would buy enormous blowtorches and incinerate the junk mail companies directly, but this is probably illegal.

The only problem with the incineration plan is that it would also destroy the occasional piece of actual mail. I got a piece of actual mail the other day, from the White House. It was signed by a machine that had learned how to reproduce the signature of Anne Higgins, Director of Presidential Correspondence, and it said: "On behalf of President Reagan, I would like to thank you for your message and to let you know that he appreciates the time you have taken to send in your views. They have been fully noted."

This letter troubles me greatly, because I never sent

any views to the White House. This means the White House now possesses somebody else's views masquerading as mine, and, what is worse, has fully noted them, whatever *that* means. I guess they have a machine in the White House basement that fully notes views at a high rate of speed, then tells the Anne Higgins signature machine to shoot out a thank you letter.

Now here's my problem: I recently acquired a view that I *would* like to send to the White House, only I'm afraid that now it won't be fully noted, because they probably have some rule about how many views will be noted per citizen per year. So I want the person who used my name to send in his view to now use *his* name to send in *my* view, and we'll be even.

My view concerns the neutron bomb, which, at the Pentagon's urging, President Reagan recently decided to build, and which would eventually be deployed in Western Europe. The neutron bomb is a nuclear device that kills people without destroying buildings. Many people feel this is inhumane; they much prefer the old-fashioned humane-type nuclear devices that kill people *and* destroy buildings.

Western Europe's reaction to the neutron bomb has been mixed: most buildings are for it, and most people are against it, on the grounds that it might kill them. They're always wallowing in sentiment, those Western Europeans.

Anyway, here's my view: I think we should develop the neutron bomb, but instead of using it to defend a bunch of ungrateful people with un-American views, we should keep it for ourselves. All we have to do is modify the design so that instead of leaving buildings alone and destroying people, it leaves buildings *and* people alone but destroys third-class mail. This would save the country billions of dollars in blowtorch fuel alone.

49

The Leak Detectors

I THINK PRESIDENT REAGAN has come up with a swell idea in his plan to give lie-detector tests to government employees suspected of leaking. "Leaking" is when a government employee tells the public what the government is doing. This is very bad, particularly in the area of foreign policy, because our foreign policy is supposed to be a secret. This principle was perfected by Richard Nixon, who used to keep the foreign policy hidden in a little jar buried in the White House lawn. Nobody ever had the vaguest notion what he was going to do next. For example, he went around for years announcing that our foreign policy was to hate the Chinese, then one day he showed up in China laughing and chatting with Chairman Mao and spilling ceremonial wine on himself. This kind of erratic behavior kept the other nations on their toes, because they could never really be sure that Dick wasn't going to suddenly turn around and, say, order the Air Force to defoliate Wales.

Today, our foreign policy is so secret that not even the President really knows what it is, which is why he is concerned about leaks. He doesn't want to be embarrassed at a press conference when some smart-mouth reporter asks him a question about why we're secretly sending arms to one of those humid little countries in Central America that the forces of international communism are always trying to spread into, and he doesn't know the answer. So the President came up with this plan whereby if the public ever gets hold of any classified government documents, which basically means all government documents except the Zip Code directory and those cretin newsletters your congressman sends you at your expense, the government employees who could have leaked the information will have to take lie-detector tests, and if it turns out they are guilty they will be fired or shot or something.

Needless to say, the American Civil Liberties Union, an organization of left-wing Communists, claimed Reagan's plan is unconstitutional, but this is typical. The ACLU is always yakking about the Constitution, and most of us are getting mighty tired of it. I mean, if the Constitution is so great, how come it was amended so many times? Huh?

Personally, I think the President's idea is excellent. My only concern is who's going to administer the lie-detector tests. We don't want government employees doing it, because they'd mess it up somehow. It would wind up like one of those Army Corps of Engineers projects where they're trying to irrigate four beet farms in Texas but they end up causing most of Iowa to be washed into the Gulf of Mexico.

So I think we should turn the lie-detecting operation over to the Private Sector, by which I mean F. Lee Bailey, the famous criminal trial lawyer who is widely considered to be extremely brilliant despite the fact that he always gives me the impression he's coated with a thin layer of slime. Bailey has this television show called "Lie Detector," wherein famous people such as Ronald Reagan's barber take lie-detector tests, then, in the highly dramatic climax, Bailey oozes up and reveals the results. I think this would be an appropriate forum for investigating suspected leakers:

BAILEY: Mr. Carbuncle, you're Assistant Secretary of State for Really Pathetic Little Countries, is that correct?

CARBUNCLE: Yes.

BAILEY: Okay, here's an innocent question to put you at ease. How are you?

CARBUNCLE: Fine, thank you.

BAILEY: Are you the person who told the *New York Times* about the secret CIA plan to drop 250,000 poison attack frogs on left-wing guerrillas in the republic of Belize?

CARBUNCLE: No.

BAILEY: Mr. Carbuncle, our polygraph machine, which has been monitoring your pulse rate and blood pressure, indicates that you are telling the truth. Either that or you have just suffered a massive heart attack. Here's an autographed picture of the President grooming his horse, and thanks a million for being our guest on "Lie Detector." Folks, be sure to stay tuned, because next we're going to see if we can figure out who leaked the plan to sell nuclear bazookas to rival street gangs in the South Bronx.

States for Sale, Cheap

FOR MORE THAN A YEAR NOW, President Reagan and the Congress have been working very hard on reducing government spending, so it should come as no surprise to anybody that they have managed to increase it. This is because the atmosphere in Washington, D.C., tends to lower people's intelligence. You've probably noticed this. You elect all these sharp people, full of brilliant ideas, and you send them to Washington, and after a few months of breathing the atmosphere they start behaving like brain-damaged turnips. As soon as they leave Washington, their IQs start to rise again.

This is why congressmen go on so many trips. Each congressman has a herd of aides who watch him constantly, and as soon as he starts to drool, or forgets how to put on his pants, the aides send him off to Switzerland or someplace on a so-called fact-finding mission, which is really just a desperate attempt to get him away from Washington long enough to boost his IQ back to the level of, say, a cocker spaniel's. The President has the same problem, which is why he almost always gets packed off to Camp David during times of international tension. His aides are afraid that if they leave him in Washington, he'll start babbling into the hot line and set off World War III.

The problem is that the only place where the President and the Congress can work on economic problems is Washington, because the economy is stored there, in a large Treasury Building vault. This means that the longer they work on the budget, the worse it gets. So the solution to our budget problems will have to come from someone who spends very little time in Washington, someone whose brain has not been affected by the atmosphere. Me, for example.

I have been thinking about the budget for several minutes now, and I believe I have come up with an excellent way to reduce it and maybe raise some money to boot. Here's my plan: *We can sell excess states.*

The way I see it, we have far too many states, many of them serving no useful purpose whatsoever. I first noticed this some years ago when my wife and I drove from Pennsylvania to Colorado. It took us practically forever to get there, mainly because there were all these flat, boring states in the way. Take Kansas. Kansas just sits there, taking up an enormous amount of space that you are required to drive across if you want to get to

Colorado. Fortunately, the Stuckey's Corporation has been thoughtful enough to locate a restaurant roughly every eighty miles along Interstate 70, so we were able to stop and buy cute little gift boxes containing a dozen miniature pecan pies, which is just enough pecan pies to keep two people occupied until the next Stuckey's so they don't go insane with boredom and drive off the interstate at speeds approaching a hundred miles per hour, threatening both human and animal life. Not that there was all that much visible life in Kansas.

Now don't get me wrong. I have nothing against Kansas persons. I'm sure that, wherever they are, they're a fun bunch. I'm just saying we can save a lot of money, and make it much easier for people to get from Pennsylvania to Colorado, if we sell Kansas and move the Kansas persons to, say, Iowa, which looks a lot like Kansas (only narrower) and seems to have plenty of extra space.

Another thing. I see no reason why we need both a North *and* a South Dakota. One Dakota ought to be sufficient. My personal opinion is that we should sell South Dakota, because the capital is called "Pierre," but I'm willing to leave the final decision up to the Congress. I'm just saying one of them should go. We should also try to sell California and New York, of course, but I doubt anybody would be stupid enough to buy them.

Another thing. If we sold some states, we'd have fewer state legislatures. I have never really understood why we have state legislatures in the first place. If they're not raising their salaries, they're arguing over some lunatic law nobody ever asked for. For example, in my state, Pennsylvania, the legislature is *obsessed* with Official State Things. Our legislators have named an Official State Animal; an Official State Bird; an Official

State Dog (it's the Great Dane, and God alone knows why); an Official State Fish; an Official State Flower; and an Official State Tree. They have even named an Official State *Insect*. I'm not kidding. It's the firefly. What does all this mean? Does it mean that if you squash a firefly in Pennsylvania, official state agents will track you down, using Great Danes, and arrest you?

I don't know the answers to these questions. All I know is that the state insect, as well as the state legislature, would become someone else's problem if we sold Pennsylvania. So I'm all for it. I'd be perfectly happy to move to Iowa, along with the Kansas persons. My only concern is that my plan might be a bit tough on the folks at Stuckey's, who make a terrific pecan pie.

There Auto B e a Law

I THINK WE Americans ought to go right out and buy some American cars. Nobody has bought an American car since 1977, and this has had profoundly negative effects on the nation, the main one being a lot of whiny television commercials:

"Hi, I'm Telly Savalas, here to tell you that under Ford's desperate new program, you don't have to pay for maintenance and repairs. In fact, you don't even have to pay for the car, or drive it, or anything. All you have to do is sign a piece of paper stating that if you were going to buy a car, it might conceivably be a Ford."

Unless we want to see more of this kind of thing, we're going to have to buy some American cars pronto. Most of us could use new cars anyway. My wife and I have been driving the same cars for more than five years, and they're starting to get a little rank, especially the one the dog threw up in on the way to the veterinarian's office. The other one, which we use to cart our nineteen-month-old son around in, smells a little better, but it has ninety billion cracker crumbs permanently bonded to the backseat by hardened saliva.

Also, we have a lot of junk in the glove compartment, mostly in the form of a series of recall letters from the manufacturer:

• *July 3, 1987:* "Dear Mr. Barry: Under the terms of United States Department of Transportation Regulation 2394754B, we are required to notify you that there exists the possibility of a potential radiation condition with respect to the wireless receiver installed in certain of our automobiles at the time of manufacture, and owners of said vehicles are therefore requested to contact their authorized sales representative with respect to an adjustment of the aforementioned potential possible condition described heretofore."

• *February 4, 1988:* "Dear Mr. Barry: A review of our records indicates that you have not responded to our earlier recall notice with respect to the potential radiation danger from the radio in your car. Your prompt attention to this matter would be appreciated."

• *October 8, 1988:* "Dear Mr. Barry: Please bring your car to the dealer right away and don't turn on the radio because you will get very sick and all your hair will fall off."

• *June 17, 1989*: "Dear Mr. Barry: If you are still alive, do *not* bring your car or yourself anywhere near the dealer. Instead, leave the car in a lightly populated area and flee on foot. We'll try to detonate it with helicopter-mounted bazookas."

So FAR, we haven't responded to the recall campaign because we've been fairly busy, and besides, we like the convenience of being able to locate our car in darkened parking lots by the glow. But I think we're going to get a new car, because we want to get Telly off the air and receive a large sum of money in the form of a rebate. In fact, we may buy several cars and retire.

If you want to buy a car, you should know that under federal law you are now required to get one with front-wheel drive. The advantage of front-wheel drive is that it's good in the snow, so when there's a really bad storm you'll be able to get to work while your neighbors are stuck home drinking bourbon by the fire. The disadvantage of front-wheel drive is that it was invented by European communists, so nobody in the United States has the vaguest notion of how it works. In fact, most mechanics have a great deal of difficulty even finding it, because it's all mixed in with the engine, which in turn is very difficult to find because it is covered with a thick layer of emissions-control objects that are designed to prevent the engine from starting, thereby drastically reducing the amount of emissions it can emit. These controls were mandated by the federal government and Ralph Nader, who drives a 1957 Pontiac with racing tires and an enormous engine.

Speaking of engines, you should also decide whether you want a regular engine or a diesel engine (named for its inventor, Rudolf Engine). Lately, a lot of people have been choosing diesel engines. I won't go into the reasons here, because, frankly, I don't know what they are. I'm just assuming there must be some really terrific reasons for paying extra money for an engine that gives off a foul odor and is extremely slow.

If you get a diesel, you'll have to learn to keep your

momentum up, the way truck drivers do. If a truck driver starts accelerating when he leaves New York, he does not hit fifty-five miles per hour until he gets to Cleveland, so he will run over anything in his path— fallen trees, passenger cars, small villages—to avoid losing his momentum.

The only other thing to consider when you buy a car is gas mileage. To make it easy for you to compare, the government requires car manufacturers to provide two mileage estimates and inform you that:

• You should pay no attention to one of the estimates, and

• You shouldn't pay much attention to the other estimate, either.

The manufacturer is also required to tell you that neither estimate applies to California. When you get right down to it, almost nothing applies to California.

You'll Look Radiant

LET'S LOOK AT the positive side of nuclear war. One big plus is that the Postal Service says it has a plan to deliver the mail after the war, which is considerably more than it is doing now. I, for one, look forward to the day after the missiles hit, when the postal person comes striding up and hands me a Publishers Clearing House Sweepstakes letter announcing that I may have already won my Dream Vacation Home, which I will probably need because my regular home will be glowing like a movie marquee.

The Postal Service isn't the only outfit that's all set for a nuclear war. The whole federal government has elaborate plans to keep doing whatever it does. As soon

58

as word arrives that enemy missiles are on the way, all the vital government officials will be whisked by helicopter to a secret mountain hideout guarded by heavily armed men. The guards are there, of course, to shoot nonvital citizens who attempt to get into the hideout, because they would get in the way of the officials who are trying to protect them.

To determine which officials are vital enough to go to the hideout, the government periodically sends out a questionnaire:

TO: *All Top Government Officials*
FROM: *The Government*
SUBJECT: *Who Gets to Go to the Secret Nuclear Hideout. Please circle the statement below that best describes how vital you are. Be as sincere as possible.*
1. *I am extremely vital and should be whisked away, in the first helicopter if possible.*
2. *I am not all that vital and should be left to die a horrible death with the ordinary citizens.*

Using the results of this questionnaire, the government has determined that all of its top officials are vital. This means, of course, that conditions in the hideout will be fairly cramped. But that is one of the prices you pay for being a public servant.

Once the officials are in the hideout, they will immediately swing into emergency action. The President will announce his emergency plan for getting the nation back on its feet, and within minutes the leader of the opposition party will hold an emergency press conference to announce that the President's plan is unfair to either middle-class taxpayers or the poor, depending on which party is the opposition at the time.

Meanwhile, Pentagon officials will warn that the surviving Russians are probably stockpiling large rocks with the intention of coming over here on crude rafts and throwing them at us. The Pentagon will recommend that we, too, start stockpiling large rocks; this will lead to an emergency tax increase.

So the government is well prepared to continue governing after a nuclear attack. The only potential fly in the ointment is that the public will probably be too sick or dead to pay taxes or receive mail. So to make sure that the government still has somebody to govern, it is the patriotic duty of all of us nonvital citizens to come up with our own personal nuclear-survival plans.

I have some experience in this area, because in 1953, when I was a first-grader at the Wampus Elementary School in Armonk, N.Y., we used to practice surviving a nuclear attack. Our technique was to go into the hall and crouch against the walls for about ten minutes. This worked extremely well, and I recommend that all of you develop emergency plans to get to Wampus Elementary as soon as you get word that the missiles are coming.

The best way to get information during a nuclear war is to listen to the Emergency Broadcast Radio Network, which is the organization that broadcasts those tests all the time:

ANNOUNCER:This is a test. For the next thirty seconds, you will hear an irritating, high-pitched squeal. We here at the Emergency Broadcast Network are bored to death, waiting for a real nuclear war, so for the past few years we've been varying the pitch of the squeal just a little bit every time. Our theory is that if we find just the right pitch, it will drive certain species of birds insane with sexual desire. We know we're getting close, because during our last test a Cleveland man carrying one of those enormous portable radios turned up real loud was pecked to death by more than three hundred lusting pigeons.

FRANKLY, I have always wondered what the Emergency Broadcast Network would broadcast if we actually had a war. I imagine they'd try to keep it upbeat, so people wouldn't get too depressed:

ANNOUNCER: Hi there! You're listening to the Emergency Broadcast Network, so don't touch that dial! It's probably melted anyway, ha ha! Weatherwise, we're expecting afternoon highs of around 6,800 degrees, followed by a cooling trend as a cloud consisting of California and Oregon blots out the sun. In the headlines, the President and key members of Congress met in an emergency breakfast this morning, and a flock of huge mutant radioactive mosquitoes has emerged from the Everglades and is flying toward New Orleans at speeds approaching four hundred miles an hour. We'll have the details in a moment, but first here's consumer affairs reporter Debbi Terri Suzi Dinkle with the first part of her eighteen-part report entitled "Radiation and You."

DINKLE: Radiation. You can't see it. You can't smell it. You can't hear it. Yet it's all over the place, and it can kill you or make your hair fall out. In my next report, we'll explore the reasons why

SO WE'LL be in good shape after the war. And there are advantages I haven't even talked about, such as that the Miss America Pageant will probably be postponed for a couple of years at least.

Caution: Government at Work

I'VE BEEN SEEING these television commercials lately in which Tug McGraw, the noted nutritionist and left-handed relief pitcher, points out in a very cheerful manner that many major soft drinks contain caffeine. Tug is concerned about this, because caffeine is one of the many substances that have been shown to cause laboratory experiments involving rats.

Tug implies we'd all be better off if we drank 7-Up, which does not contain caffeine. He neglects to point out that 7-Up contains sugar, which, as you are no doubt aware, usually causes instant death. But I can't blame Tug for forgetting to warn us about sugar: nobody can keep up with all the things you're not supposed to eat and drink, because scientists come up with new ones all the time.

You young readers should feel very fortunate to live in an era in which we know how dangerous everything is. When I was a child, people thought everything was safe except communism, smutty books, and tobacco, and a lot of people weren't sure about tobacco. For example, the cigarette manufacturers thought tobacco was fine, and as a public service they ran many advertisements in which attractive persons offered thoughtful scientific arguments in favor of smoking, such as: "Luckies separate the men from the boys . . . but not from the girls," and "Winston tastes good, like a cigarette should."

But then the U.S. Surgeon General, who is the highest-ranking surgeon in the Army, decided that cigarettes are bad for people, and recommended that the manufacturers put little warnings on cigarette packs.

Congressmen from tobacco-growing states offered to help with the wording, so at first the warning was a bit vague:

NOTE—The U.S. Surgeon General thinks that cigarettes could possibly be somewhat less than ideal in terms of your health, but of course he could be wrong.

But over the years the warning has gotten stronger, so now it says:

WARNING—Cigarettes will kill you, you stupid jerk.

These days the government won't even allow cigarette manufacturers to advertise on television. All you see are those public health commercials in which smug ten-year-old girls order you not to smoke, to the point where you want to rush right out and inhale an entire pack of unfiltered Camels just for spite.

Some of you may be wondering why the same government that goes around warning people not to smoke also subsidizes farmers who grow tobacco. The answer is that the government is afraid that if it stops paying the farmers to grow tobacco, they'll start doing something even worse, such as growing opium or beating crippled children with baseball bats. So the government figures the wisest course is to pay them to grow tobacco, then warn people not to smoke it.

The antismoking campaign was such a hit that the government decided to investigate the chemicals that make diet soft drinks taste sweet. Researchers wearing white laboratory coats filled a huge vat with Diet Coke and dropped rats into it from a sixty-foot-high catwalk, and they noticed that most of the rats died, some before they even reached the vat. So the government banned the chemicals, but the diet-soda manufacturers immediately developed new ones, which also failed the vat test. At this point, the government realized that the manufacturers could come up with chemicals as fast as it could ban them, and that at the rate things were going the country would face a major rat shortage. So the government decided to let the manufacturers keep their chemicals, but it ordered them to put a little warning on diet soft drink containers that says: "Do not put this product in a big vat and drop rats into it from a catwalk."

Nowadays, Warning the Public is a major industry. Every schoolchild knows the hazards associated with cigarettes, caffeine, diet soft drinks, sugar, alcohol, dairy products, nondairy products, electronic games, air, league bowling, and chemicals in general. Any day now, you'll pick up the newspaper and read:

BOSTON—Laboratory scientists at a very major scientific university announced today that everything is terribly, terribly dangerous. Dr. Creston I. Posthole, who headed the research project, said scientists got a bunch of rats and just let them lead normal lives—eating, drinking, sleeping, watching television, making appointments, etc. "They all died within a matter of days," reported Dr. Posthole. "Most of them had cancer. Some of them also had irregular bowel movements." Dr. Posthole said the scientists weren't sure what the study proved, but they feel the government ought to do something about it.

Until we get that Final Warning, we'll all have to make do as best we can. I, for one, plan to consume nothing but filtered rainwater. For amusement, I may take a chance on some smutty books.

64

Taxation Without Reservation

A Taxing Proposal

HERE IT IS AGAIN, income tax time, and I imagine many of you readers, especially the ones with smaller brains, are eagerly awaiting my annual tax-advice column. Those of you who were fortunate enough to read last year's column no doubt recall that I advised you to cheat, on the grounds that by reducing the amount of money you gave the government, you'd be supporting President Reagan in his program to reduce government spending. I'm proud to report that many of you went all out to support the President, and I'm sure he'd thank you personally if the Secret Service allowed him to visit federal prisons.

But this year we have an entirely new plan, taxwise. This year, President Reagan needs all the money he can get, because he was going over the figures recently with his aides, Huey, Dewey, and Louie, and they noticed that the government was going to be short by something like $200 billion. "Gosh," chuckled the President. "That's even bigger than those humongous deficits the Democrats used to run up when I went around making fun of them on the radio! Why, for all the difference I've made in the past two years, the nation might just as well have had Ted Kennedy as president! Or a toaster!" Then they all had a good laugh and decided to jack up taxes. The other option, of course, was to cut government spending, but they rejected that because they have already cut spending to the bone in the form of raising it by about $100 billion a year.

The Democrats are happy as clams about raising taxes. The Democrats believe that if God did not want them to raise taxes, He would not have created the Internal Revenue Service. So finally, after two years of bickering, the President and the Democrats are beginning to see eye-to-eye on the importance of taking money away from the public. Recently, for example, the Democrats supported the President's plan to have a new gasoline tax under which the government will take $50 billion from motorists such as yourself. This will create jobs. See, if you were allowed to keep the money, you wouldn't create jobs with it. You'd just throw it into the bushes or something. But the government will spend it, thereby creating jobs. In this case, the government will spend the $50 billion on a major road-repair program, including several million dollars for highway construction signs that say:

CONGRESSMAN ROBERT "BOB" LUNGER
and the United States Department of Transportation are pleased to announce that for the next 86.8 miles there will be federal traffic cones all over the place and hundreds of friends and relatives of a contractor who contributed to the campaign of
CONGRESSMAN ROBERT "BOB" LUNGER
standing around with red flags, and directing traffic so casually that they may occasionally wave your car right into an oncoming tractor-trailer loaded with propane gas, so we regret the inconvenience, but as
CONGRESSMAN ROBERT "BOB" LUNGER
pointed out when he flew in by federal helicopter to make a speech taking credit for this $364.7 million highway-repair project, we cannot allow our nation's highways to deteriorate, especially the ones that provide access to land owned by
CONGRESSMAN ROBERT "BOB" LUNGER

Thank you.

BUT THE $50 BILLION won't be nearly enough to allow Congress to create jobs on the scale it would like. And on top of that, President Reagan needs money to buy additional exploding devices to defend you with. So what can you, the ordinary taxpayer, do to help? Here's what: This year, when you prepare your income tax return, I want you to lie in the government's favor. I want you to declare more income than you actually received, and I want you to deliberately fail to report large numbers of legitimate deductions.

Some of you will be caught, of course. Some of you may be called in to face IRS audits. You may even be forced to accept a large refund, thus depriving the government of money it could have used for your benefit. These risks are unavoidable, but they can be minimized if a few of us continue to cheat, so the IRS will be less likely to see any particular pattern. I'm willing to volunteer to be one of the few. It's a dirty job, but somebody has to do it.

Our Patriotic Booty

I SAY WE ALL HELP President Reagan cut government waste. I say we cheat on our income taxes this year.

I mean, let's face it: the reason the government wastes hundreds of billions of dollars is that we *give* it hundreds of billions of dollars. Even an intelligent organization would have trouble spending that much money usefully; the government can't even come close. So it ends up spending money on things like the Office for Micronesian Status Negotiations. I am serious.

According to the Congressional Directory, one of the things the government spends your money on is an office devoted to negotiating the status of Micronesia. I'm not saying its employees are goofing off: I'm sure they get up early in the morning, negotiate the status of Micronesia all day, then come home and collapse. I'm just saying that if they haven't been able to get Micronesia straightened out after all these years, then the hell with Micronesia.

Now I know President Reagan has promised to comb through the budget and get rid of everything we don't need except nuclear weapons, but I seriously doubt he'll ever even *notice* the Office for Micronesian Status Negotiations, let alone the International Pacific Halibut Commission. You didn't know we had a Halibut Commission, did you? Well, we do. It's in Seattle, Washington. When the folks at the Halibut Commission answer the phone, they say: "Good morning, Halibut Commission." They're just as bold as brass about it. No shame whatsoever. They know Ron will never find out about them, and even if he does, some congressman will claim the Halibut Commission is *vital* and therefore needs the support of all taxpayers, including the ones who live in Kentucky and don't even like halibut. And then some *other* congressman will say: "Well, if you're going to keep the Halibut Commission, *I'm* going to keep the Inter-American Tropical Tuna Commission." Before long, the budget will be bigger than it was when Ron started to cut it.

So let's help Ron out: let's keep the money out of the government's hands altogether. Let's each claim an extra thirty or forty dependents on our tax returns this year. We should view it as our patriotic duty, sort of like buying war bonds.

Another patriotic thing we can do is send Ron lists of government activities we do not want to pay for anymore. The top item on my list is newsletters from congressmen: The way I see it, we taxpayers have an agreement with our congressmen: we give them a hundred thousand dollars a year each and offices and staffs and traveling expenses and cheap hair cuts and subsidized dining rooms and other privileges, and in return they go away for two years. If we valued them or their opinions, we never would have voted to send them away in the first place. The *last* thing we want them to do is clutter up our mailboxes with accounts of their activities:

Dear 647th Congressional District Resident:

I'm just taking a minute out from my hectic schedule down here in the nation's capital to let you know that my schedule down here is very hectic. As a member of the House Joint Plumbing Committee's Ad Hoc Subcommittee on Spigots and Drains, I recently went on a two-week Special Fact-Finding Mission to Rio de Janeiro. Here's the fact I found: In the Southern Hemisphere, water goes down the drain in a clockwise direction, whereas in the Northern Hemisphere, which includes the 647th Congreddional District, water goes down the drain in a counterclockwise direction. Or else it's the other way around. Next month, I plan to go to Argentina to determine which way water goes down the drain there, and whether any of this is related to the spread of International Communism.

All the best,
Congressman Bob Bugpit

Here are some other government activities I don't

want to pay for anymore:

• National weeks and months, as in National Seedless Prune Week or National Faucet Repair Month.
• All programs that are administered by people whose titles contain more than three words. Take, for example, the National Science Foundation's Division of Engineering. The *Division Director, Physics,* could stay, because his title contains just three words. But the *Division Director, Division of Polar Programs,* would be given two weeks to clear out his or her desk and find useful work. And the *Executive Assistant, Planning and Evaluation, Biological, Behavioral and Social Sciences,* would be taken out and shot.

Taxpayer's Blues

I AM BEGINNING to suspect that many of your big-time Washington national news reporters have coleslaw for brains. My evidence is that for the past few months they have been telling us that the Reagan administration and the Congress are busy reducing government spending. You can't pick up a newspaper or turn on a television newscast without reading or hearing about all these drastic budget cuts. If you were a very stupid person, you might get the impression that the administration and the Congress really *are* reducing government spending. This, of course, is utterly ridiculous.

The big-time Washington national news reporters evidently have fallen into the obvious trap of believing that politicians actually intend to do what they say they intend to do. Administration officials say they intend to reduce government spending. Most senators say *they* intend to reduce government spending. And most members of the House of Representatives say they, too, intend to reduce government spending. Only a fool would conclude that they intend to do anything but increase government spending.

And they will increase it. No matter what budget they end up adopting, next year the government will spend more money, and collect more taxes, than it does this year. If you don't believe me, look it up.

What happened is that just before he left office, Jimmy Carter (remember Jimmy Carter?) proposed to increase the federal budget *enormously.* Then along came Ronald Reagan, the Taxpayer's Friend, the Foe of Big Government. Ron decided to replace Jimmy's enormous budget increase with one that was merely huge. So for the last few months, the politicians have been arguing over whether to increase the budget enormously or just hugely. The news media refer to this process as "cutting" the budget.

The best way to understand this whole issue is to look at what the government does: it takes money away from some people, keeps a bunch of it, and gives the rest to other people. This means there are two kinds of people in the United States:

• People who pay more to the government than they get from it (taxpayers);

• People who get more from the government than they pay to it (senators, welfare recipients, cabinet members, defense contractors, government employees, et cetera.)

So if you are just a plain old ordinary taxpayer, the

Great Budget Debate doesn't really concern you. One way or another, the government is going to spend more of your money; the only real issue is who is going to get it.

For the past forty years, the government preferred to use your money for Social Programs. Most of these are aimed at Helping the Poor. Now the problem poor people have is obvious: they don't have enough money. They can't afford food, housing, or medical care. The simple, obvious, efficient way for the government to help them is to give them money so they can buy these things. So that is not how the government does it.

See, if the government merely gave money to poor people, no matter how inefficiently it did it, it would need only one bureaucracy. This would force a lot of people to leave government employment and find honest work. So instead of simply giving money to poor people, the government Administers Programs for them. You've got your food programs. You've got your housing programs. You've got your medical care programs. And so on. This way you get lots of administrators. You also guarantee that poor people remain poor, since they're so busy being administered they don't have time to work. This is fine with the poverty-program administrators; the worst possible thing that could happen to them is for poor people to stop being poor. If that happened, the administrators would have nothing to administer. But fortunately, poverty has continued; in fact, it has been a major growth industry. A lot of people have made very good livings Helping the Poor.

Then along came Ronald Reagan. Ron believes taxpayers are tired of having their money taken away and used for massive, inefficient Social Programs. He wants to take their money away and use it for massive, inefficient defense programs. So the poverty-program administrators are extremely unhappy, while the defense-program administrators are tickled pink. But they have the same problem the social-program administrators had: they have to figure out how to spend the extra billions on defense without actually making the country any safer, because if they really *do* make it safer, they won't be able to demand more money.

This is tough, because the United States is obviously not directly threatened except by Russian missiles, and we already have enough missiles to blow up the whole world if the Russians ever attack us. So the defense-program administrators have come up with a very imaginative plan: they have decided to defend virtually every country in the world other than Russia and its allies. Since most of these countries are hopelessly unstable, we could spend every dollar every taxpayer ever earns to defend them and never come close to succeeding. But the defense-program administrators will certainly be busy.

Right now, for example, they are busily administering the defense of El Salvador, a wretched little country that has suddenly become Vital to Our National Security. According to many people familiar with El Salvador, including a former U.S. ambassador there, the El Salvadoran government spends much of its time shooting El Salvadorans. But our government is sending them arms anyway. I mean, it has to do *something* with the money. Anything but let taxpayers keep it.

The Media Is the Mess-up

Perking Up the News

ONE SWELL THING about the United States is that newspapers can print whatever stories they want. Another one is that nobody has to read them.

In the United States, the press is protected by the First Amendment to the Constitution, which states: "Thou shalt not covet thy neighbor's wife." No, wait, that's the Ten Commandments. Anyway, whatever the Constitution says about the press, we Americans should be darned glad it says it. In the Soviet Union, the press is controlled by the official news agency, Tass, which is always giving out highly amusing versions of world events:

MOSCOW—Tass, the official Soviet news agency, announced today that Soviet troops have entered Poland, Czechoslovakia, Hungary, Iran, Albania, Mongolia, Egypt, Norway, and Saskatchewan at the request of "liberation movements fighting the Western capitalist colonialist Zionist hegemony of running-dog plague-carrying widow-stabbing baby-eating lackeys of United Stales imperialism." Tass said the Soviet forces will ride around in nuclear-powered tanks until the various countries are safe from the threat of further oppression.

I imagine the Russian people regard Tass as a major chuckle. I bet they can't *wait* to see the paper each day, so they can read what isn't going on in the rest of the world. In fact, this is the big advantage their system has over ours: since the Russian government always lies, the people can safely assume that the opposite of whatever Tass says is true. Over here, things are more complicated. Our government lies a lot, too, but it can't force the newspapers to print the lies accurately. From time to time the reporters try to get at the truth, and once in a great while they succeed. So you can be *fairly* sure you're reading lies, but, unlike the Russians, you can never really *count* on it. The only reliable parts of American newspapers are horoscopes, weather forecasts, and economic outlooks, which are all consistently false.

Another problem with American newspapers is that they are positively *obsessed* with boring issues. Take the Helsinki Accords. *You* don't care about the Helsinki Accords, and neither does any other normal person. You can go into every bar and shopping center in America, and you will never once hear anyone say: "Hey, how about them Helsinki Accords?" But newspapers will drone on and on about them at the slightest provocation.

Newspapers are also inordinately fond of writing about statements by presidential press secretaries. No presidential press secretary in the history of the United States has ever said anything newsworthy. I mean, his whole *job* is to make sure nobody has the vaguest idea what the President is thinking. Nevertheless, every morning dozens of Washington reporters troop into the press secretary's office and write down everything he says:

PRESS SECRETARY: I wish to correct the accounts that appeared in some newspapers yesterday quoting me as stating that the President's mood is one of Restrained Optimism. I did not state that. I stated that the President's mood is one of Guarded Optimism.

REPORTER: Does this represent a change in the President's mood?

PRESS SECRETARY: It does not represent a change from yesterday. The President has been in a consistently Guardedly Optimistic mood for two days now.

Now at this point, your average citizen would be asleep. But the Washington reporters think this stuff is *dynamite.* They're wetting their *pants* over the President's mood. They all go roaring out to find some presidential aide, who tells them, in strictest confidence, that despite what the press secretary would have them believe, the President's mood is actually one of Hopeful Caution.

The next day all the papers run page-one presidential-mood stories long enough to choke Brahma bulls. The reporters read them. The President's aides read them. Everybody else, including the President, turns directly to the sports section.

I think British newspapers have a much better approach. They ignore the official actions of the government, which hasn't done anything in forty years anyway, and focus on something readers can respond to: sex. If you read the headlines in British newspapers, you get the impression that everybody in the government, with the possible exception of the Queen, is a pervert:

EIGHT MEMBERS OF PARLIAMENT ARRESTED IN BED WITH NEWTS

This is the kind of story you can sink your *teeth* into, so to speak. I'd like to see American newspapers try the same sort of thing on the Reagan administration. Let's face it: the Reagan administration is full of really boring-looking guys, guys who have investment portfolios and matching-pen-and-pencil sets. If the newspapers write about what these guys *say*, the entire country will be asleep in a matter of weeks. People will be nodding off at work, in their cars, at the controls of commercial airliners. The country will collapse. The newspapers should see it as their *duty* to print stories about high-level sex. They wouldn't even have to lie:

WASHINGTON—An in-depth examination of the statements of Vice President George Bush reveals he had never publicly denied having spent two weeks in a motel with a lawn tractor.

Imagine seeing *that* in, say, the *New York Times.* It would turn the country around. People would start to care about public affairs again.

Junkyard Journalism

I BET YOU DON'T READ the *National Enquirer,* or any of the other publications sold at supermarket checkout counters. I bet you think these publications are written for people with the intellectual depth of shrubs, people who need detailed, written instructions to put their shoes on correctly. Well, you're missing a lot. I have taken to reading checkout-counter publications, and I have picked up scads of useful information. For example, a recent *Enquirer* issue contains a story headlined WHATEVER HAPPENED TO THE CAST OF "THE FLYING NUN"? Now here is a vital story most of the so-called big-time newspapers didn't have the guts to print. I mean, while the *New York Times* and the *Washington Post* were frittering away their space on stories about Alexander Haig, millions of people all over America were tossing and turning at night, wondering what happened to the cast of "The Flying Nun." All over the country, you'd see little knots of people huddling together and asking each other: "Remember Marge Redmond, who played Sister Jacqueline in 'The Flying Nun'? Whatever happened to her?"

Well, the *Enquirer* has the answer. Somehow, an *Enquirer* reporter got Marge's agent to reveal that Marge has appeared in commercials for Tide, Bravo, Betty Crocker, and Ajax. "But," adds the agent, "she is perhaps best known as Sara Tucker of Sara Tucker's Inn on the Cool Whip commercials."

I, for one, was stunned by this revelation. Believe it or not, I had never made the connection between Sister Jacqueline and Sara Tucker. Now, of course, it seems obvious: only an actress skilled enough to perform in "The Flying Nun" would be able to convincingly portray a woman who is so deranged that she puts huge globs of Cool Whip on her desserts at what is supposed to be a good restaurant. But without the *Enquirer*, I would never have known.

And without the *National Examiner,* which is like the *Enquirer* except it uses even smaller words, I would never have found out that

40 VAMPIRES ROAM NORTH AMERICA

This extremely scientific story reports on the research of Dr. Stephen Kaplan, a parapsychologist who founded the Vampire Research Center. I got the impression that Dr. Kaplan *is* the Vampire Research Center, but the story never makes this clear. It also doesn't say where he got his degree in parapsychology, but we can safely assume it was someplace like Harvard.

Anyway, Dr. Kaplan sent questionnaires to people who requested mail from the center, and forty responded that, yes indeed, they are vampires. In a way, this cheered me up. I mean, I always thought of vampires as evil, uncooperative persons of Central European descent who never even file income tax returns, and here we have forty of them who cheerfully fill out questionnaires for the Vampire Research Center.

Dr. Kaplan, who (surprise!) plans to write a book about vampires, believes there are lots more vampires around. "This probably represents the tip of the vampire iceberg," he told the *Examiner*, which knows a good metaphor when it hears one. If Dr. Kaplan is correct, I imagine that before long we'll have a federal law requiring large companies to hire a certain percentage of vampires. They have been discriminated against long enough.

Here are some more stories you missed: "Bingo Can Restore the Will to Live On," "$50 Operation to Restore Virginity," "A Machine Chewed Up My Legs," "Cancer Ruins Sex," "Dead Man Thanks Killer" and "34 Years in a Haunted House." The last one is about a Massachusetts man and woman whose house is occupied by a ghost that does terrifying things, such as caressing the woman's brow with ghostly fingers when she's reading. By way of proof, the article is accompanied by an actual photograph of the woman reading.

Checkout-counter publications also perform valuable services for their readers. The *Examiner* has a psychic named Maria who uses her incredible psychic ability to answer baffling questions, such as "Dear Maria: A man I am dating keeps asking me to spank him. What should I do?" To which Maria replies: "Dump him. He's nuts."

And some people have the nerve to claim that psychics are frauds.

But the best part of checkout-counter publications is the advertisements. They can make you rich. I, for one, never realized how much money you can make stuffing envelopes, but according to the ads in the *Enquirer* and the *Examiner*, the sky is the limit. I mean, people are willing to pay you *thousands of dollars a week* to stuff envelopes. I figure there must be a catch. For one thing, they never tell you what you have to stuff the envelopes *with*. Maybe it's poison spiders. That would explain the high pay.

Another ad I saw in the *Examiner* just *intrigued* me. The headline says: JESUS IS HERE. Now I am going to quote very carefully from the ad, because otherwise you won't believe me:

Tired of money-mad ministers and physicians? Free, drugless urine cures all ills, increases energy and intelligence and is prescribed in the Bible. . . Due to its immuno-genetic qualities, urine is the only antidote for nuclear radiation . . . If you are not fully convinced that the course heralds the Second Coming of Christ, return it in perfect condition for a full refund. . .

The course costs seventy-five dollars; otherwise I would have sent for it already. I am very curious about it, and even more curious about the person who wrote it. I strongly suspect he's one of the people who responded to Dr. Kaplan's vampire survey.

Bring Back Captain Video

IF WE'RE EVER GOING to return the United States to its glory days (August 14 and 15, 1955) we're going to have to do something about television. This country has been going downhill ever since they took "The Ed Sullivan Show" off the air, and I say we should bring it back. Some of you may argue that Ed Sullivan is dead, but I don't see how that would affect his judgment or delivery in the slightest. Ed knew talent when he saw it. He discovered such acts as the little dogs that wore dresses and walked around on their hind legs for twenty or thirty minutes while the audience, whose average IQ could not have been higher than 18, roared with laughter. *That* was entertainment. If we had Ed Sullivan back, we wouldn't spend Sunday evenings being depressed by "60 Minutes":

"Good evening, I'm Mike Wallace. Tonight on '60 Minutes' we'll explain why the Earth will be covered with a sheet of ice eight miles thick within the next fifteen years; we'll talk to a government researcher who has discovered that, because of a manufacturing defect, 93 percent of the refrigerators in the United States could explode at the slightest touch; and Andy Rooney will take an amusing look at whisk brooms."

Another show we could do without is "Phil Donahue":

"Hi, and welcome to the 'Phil Donahue' show. My guest today is Wesley Snate, who was convicted in 1979 of charges that he bludgeoned roughly three hundred Los Angeles-area French poodles to death. Mr. Snate

has written a very sensitive and moving book about his experience, entitled They Deserved It, *and I have invited him on the show so I can ask him many sensitive and insightful questions so our viewing audience will gain a deeper understanding of dog bludgeoners and perhaps buy his book."*

The trouble with Phil's approach is that, with all his tiptoeing around, he hardly ever gets around to the really depraved stuff everybody is tuned in to hear. For sheer depravity, Phil's show can't hold a candle to the old "Queen for a Day" show, in which deranged housewives competed to see who had the most miserable life:

FIRST CONTESTANT: My husband had a stroke and he lost his job and our house got repossessed so we had to live under a sheet of plywood in the supermarket parking lot but when it got cold our kids got tuberculosis except the youngest who got kidney disease so we built a fire under there to keep warm but the plywood caught fire and burned up my insulin and all our clothes so I had to wrap the kids in discarded plastic garbage bags which is giving them a rash.

SECOND CONTESTANT: Well, I have cancer, of course, and my husband was hit by a truck which gave him amnesia and he wandered off and I haven't seen him since which would be okay except he had just withdrawn our life savings so we could pay for an operation for little Theodora who has lost the use of her fingers because of rat bites and can't tend little Buford's iron lung when I'm out picking through the garbage for supper.

THIRD CONTESTANT: Well my problem is that . . . arghhhhh. *(The third contestant keels over and dies.)*

Then the audience would applaud each contestant,

and the one who got the most applause would win an Amana freezer. It was a terrific show.

WE'RE ALSO GOING to have to do something about children's television. Today's children watch shows like "Sesame Street," which teaches them that the world is full of friendly interracial adults and cute puppets and letters that form recognizable patterns. This is, of course, a pack of lies. When I was a kid, in New York, my friends and I watched shows like "Captain Video," which taught us that the world was full of evil forces trying to destroy the earth, which turns out to be absolutely correct.

"Captain Video" consisted of five episodes a week, no one of which cost more than eleven dollars to produce. The episodes always took place in Captain Video's spaceship. It was an *extremely* low-budget spaceship. For example, Captain Video's radio was a regular telephone handset, except he held it as if it were a microphone and talked into the listening end.

In a typical episode, Captain Video's spaceship would be under attack by an evil alien warlord who had a robot named Tobor (get it?). The evil alien would order Tobor, who was played by a stagehand wearing cardboard boxes wrapped in aluminum foil, to attack. "Kill, Tobor, kill," he would say, and the stagehand would go lumbering toward Captain Video. Just when he got close, Captain Video would come up with this *brilliant* idea: he would say "Go back, Tobor, go back." Then the stagehand would start lumbering toward the evil alien. Then there would be some commercials. Then the alien would say "Kill, Tobor, kill," again, and the stagehand would start toward Captain Video again, and Captain Video would say "Go back, Tobor, go back" again, and there would be more commercials, and before you knew it the half hour had just flown by. Kids today don't get that kind of drama.

They also don't get Meaningful Social Lessons, the kind we got from shows about cowboys and Indians. These shows taught us that not all Indians were savage killers. For example, Tonto was a good Indian. As I recall, all the others were savage killers.

In Depth, but Shallowly

IF YOU WANT to take your mind off the troubles of the real world, you should watch local TV news shows. I know of no better way to escape reality, except perhaps heavy drinking.

Local TV news programs have given a whole new definition to the word *news*. To most people, *news* means *information about events that affect a lot of people*. On local TV news shows, *news* means *anything that you can take a picture of, especially if a local TV News Personality can stand in front of it*. This is why they are so fond of car accidents, burning buildings, and crowds: these are good for standing in front of. On the other hand, local TV news shows tend to avoid stories about things that local TV News Personalities cannot stand in front of, such as budgets and taxes and the economy. If you want to get a local TV news show to do a story on the budget, your best bet is to involve it in a car crash.

I travel around the country a lot, and as far as I can tell, virtually all local TV news shows follow the same format. First you hear some exciting music, the kind you hear in space movies, while the screen shows local TV

News Personalities standing in front of various News Events. Then you hear the announcer:

ANNOUNCER: From the On-the-Spot Action Eyewitness News Studios, this is the On-the-Spot Action Eyewitness News, featuring Anchorman Wilson Westbrook, Co-Anchorperson Stella Snape, Minority-Group Member James Edwards, Genial Sports Personality Jim Johnson, Humorous Weatherperson Dr. Reed Stevens, and Norm Perkins on drums. And now, here's Wilson Westbrook.

WESTBROOK: Good evening. Tonight from the On-the-Spot Action Eyewitness News Studios we have actual color film of a burning building, actual color film of two cars after they ran into each other, actual color film of the front of a building in which one person shot another person, actual color film of another burning building, and special reports on roller-skating and child abuse. But for the big story tonight, we go to City Hall, where On-the-Spot Reporter Reese Kernel is standing live.

KERNEL: I am standing here live in front of City Hall being televised by the On-the-Spot Action Eyewitness News minicam with Mayor Bryce Hallbread.

MAYOR: That's "Hallwood."

KERNEL: What?

MAYOR: My name is "Hallwood." You said "Hallbread."

KERNEL: Look, Hallbread, do you want to be on the news or don't you?

MAYOR: Yes, of course, it's just that my name is—

KERNEL: Listen, this is the top-rated news show in the three-county area, and if you think I have time to memorize every stupid detail, you'd better think again.

MAYOR: I'm sorry. "Hallbread" is fine, really.

KERNEL: Thank you, Mayor Hallbread. And now back to Wilson Westbrook in the On-the-Spot Action Eyewitness News Studios.

WESTBROOK: Thank you, Reese; keep us posted if anything further develops on that important story. And now, as I promised earlier, we have actual color film of various objects that either burned or crashed, which we will project on the screen behind me while I talk about them. Here is a building on fire. Here is another building on fire. Here is a car crash. This film was shot years ago, but you can safely assume that objects just like these crashed or burned in the three-county area today. And now we go to my Co-Anchorperson, Stella Snape, for a Special Report on her exhaustive three-week investigation into the problem of child abuse in the three-county area. Well, Stella, what did you find?

SNAPE: Wilson, I found that child abuse is very sad. What happens is that people abuse children. It's just awful. Here you see some actual color film of me standing in front of a house. Most of your child abuse occurs in houses. Note that I am wearing subdued colors.

WESTBROOK (reading from a script): Are any efforts under way here in the three-county area to combat child abuse?

SNAPE: Yes.

WESTBROOK: Thank you, Stella, for that informative report. On the lighter side, On-the-Spot Action Eyewitness Reporter Terri Tompkins has prepared a three-part series on roller-skating in the three-county area.

TOMPKINS: Roller-skating has become a major craze in California and the three-county area, as you can see by this actual color film of me on roller skates

91

outside the On-the-Spot Action Eyewitness News Studio. This certainly is a fun craze. Tomorrow, in Part Two of this series, we'll see actual color film of me falling down. On Wednesday we'll see me getting up.

WESTBROOK: We'll look forward to those reports. Our next story is from Minority-Group Reporter James Edwards, who, as he has for the last 324 consecutive broadcasts, spent the day in the minority-group sector of the three-county area finding out what minorities think.

EDWARDS: Wilson, I'm standing in front of a crowd of minority-group members, and as you can see, their mood is troubled. *(The crowd smiles and waves at the camera.)*

WESTBROOK: Good report, James. Well, we certainly had a sunny day here in the three-county area, didn't we, Humorous Weatherperson Dr. Reed Stevens?

STEVENS: Ha ha. We sure did, though I'm certainly troubled by that very troubling report Stella did on child abuse. But we should see continued warm weather through Wednesday. Here are a bunch of charts showing the relative humidity and stuff like that. Ha ha.

WESTBROOK: Ha ha. Well, things weren't nearly as bright on the sports scene, were they, Genial Sports Personality Jim Johnson?

JOHNSON: No, Wilson, they certainly weren't. The Three-County Community College Cutlasses lost their fourth consecutive game today. Here you see actual color footage of me watching the game from the sidelines. The disgust is evident on my face. I intended to have actual color film of me interviewing the coach after the game, but the team bus crashed and everyone was killed.

WESTBROOK: Thank you, Jim. And now, here is Basil Holp, the General Manager of KUSP-TV, to present an Editorial Viewpoint:

HOLP: The management of KUSP-TV firmly believes that something ought to be done about earthquakes. From time to time we read in the papers that an earthquake has hit some wretched little country and knocked houses down and killed people. This should not be allowed to continue. Maybe we should have a tax or something. What the heck, we can afford it. The management of KUSP-TV is rolling in money.

ANNOUNCER: The preceding was the opinion of the management of KUSP-TV People with opposing points of view are probably in the vast majority.

WESTBROOK: Well, that wraps up tonight's version of the On-the-Spot Action Eyewitness News. Tune in tonight to see essentially the same stories.

Radio's Air Heads

IF YOU DON'T LISTEN to radio talk shows, you really should, because it gives you a chance to reassure yourself that a great many people out there are much stupider than you are. Here's how these shows go:

HOST: Hi, this is "You Get to Talk on the Actual Radio," the show where You Make a Difference. I'm your host, Hubert Spankle, going under the radio name David Windsor Castle, which sounds better. Today I thought we'd talk about President Reagan's economic plan. What do you think about it? Let's go to the phones and find out. Hello, you're on the air.

CALLER: Hello, David?

HOST: This is David. Go ahead.

CALLER: Am I on the radio now?

HOST: Yes, you are. Go ahead.

CALLER: Go ahead and talk?

HOST: Yes. Go right ahead and talk

CALLER: I'm so nervous.

HOST: Don't be nervous. Go right ahead and talk. Right now. Just talk.

CALLER: Well, I just wanted to tell you what happened to my husband. He was riding the lawn mower, which we just got at Sears—can I say Sears?—well, let's just say we just got it at a major department store, and believe me it wasn't cheap, and he was driving it near the kitchen window, and all of a sudden he crashed right through the septic tank, and he disappeared right into the ground, and the firemen had to come and get him out, and I spent three hours going over the lawn tractor with Lysol—can I say Lysol?—and it still doesn't smell what you'd call attractive, not to mention my husband, and I think they ought to make those septic tanks stronger, because a lot of people have lawn tractors, and—

HOST: I certainly hear what you're saying. What do you think of President Reagan's economic plan?

CALLER: President Reagan's what?

HOST: His economic plan.

CALLER: Well, I really haven't been too involved in it, because we live in the suburbs, which is why we got the lawn tractor, but we had no idea that our septic tank—

HOST: Thanks for your views. Let's see how some of our other listeners feel about President Reagan's economic plan. Hello, you're on the air.

CALLER: Hello, Frank?

HOST: No, this is David Windsor Castle, and you're on "You Get to Talk on the Actual Radio." What's on your mind?

CALLER: What's on my mind is I'm trying to get hold of Frank, because I just found out that Denise—

HOST: Excuse me, but this is a radio show, and there is no Frank here.

CALLER: Well, when he gets there you better tell him that Denise found out about what's been going on at the Jolly Goat Motel. Somebody sent her pictures of Frank, Louella, Preston, and the trained snakes, and the last I heard Denise was buying a gun, so he'd better—

HOST: Okay, let's see if any of our other listeners have anything to add about President Reagan's economic plan. Hello, you're on the air.

CALLER: Yeah, I'm calling about that lady with the septic tank. It just so happens I make septic tanks, and there's no way you can make one collapse with just a lawn tractor unless the guy who's riding it weighs about six hundred pounds. Why didn't you ask her how much her husband weighs? I bet he's a real lard bucket. You see these guys out on their lawn tractors, flab hanging down almost to the ground, and it makes you want to puke.

HOST: Let's go to another caller. You're on the air.

CALLER: Hi. I'd like to talk about President Reagan's economic plan.

HOST: Thank God.

CALLER: It seems to me that people are being too quick to criticize the President's plan, before it has had a chance to—Oh no!

(In the background is the sound of a door lock being shot open with a .357 Magnum.)

CALLER: Denise!

(More shots, screams)

HOST: Well, that concludes today's version of "You Get to Talk on the Actual Radio." Tune in tomorrow, when

95

we'll explore the situation in the Middle East.

What to Ban on Video

I KEEP READING these stories about these towns that want to ban video arcade games, as if these games were part of the International Communist Conspiracy. You know:

POND SCUM, ARKANSAS—The town council in this small pig-farming community voted last night to ban video arcade games on the grounds that they are a threat to the moral fiber of the town's youth. "The youth in this town barely got any moral fiber left to speak of, and I blame these here video games", charged Council President Lionel B. Sparge. "When I was a youth, Pond Scum didn't have no video games, and we found plenty to do. For example, we'd stand around and spit."

I agree with the people who want to ban video games. These games definitely destroy your moral fiber. At least they destroy *my* moral fiber. I have this video game that I play all the time on my personal home computer, which I keep back in a back bedroom. I don't allow my two-year-old son to get near it, because it might destroy his moral fiber, and also he tends to pull the plug right when I'm in an important phase of my game, such as when the aliens materialize out of hyperspace.

So what has happened is that my son has been going through all these critical stages of growth and development out in the living room, and I've missed most of it. Not that I mind all that much, really, since if you want to participate in my son's growth and development you have to read him these profoundly dull children's books with names like *Let's Go to a Condiments Factory* and *Tommy the Toad Vacuums the Carpet.* So I've left his development pretty much in the hands of my wife, with instructions that she should call me if he reaches any new developmental stages so I can come out to the living room and watch him for a few minutes.

And I'm not the only one whose moral fiber is being destroyed. It is a proven scientific fact that video games are also corrupting American youth. In a recent experiment, scientific researchers exposed a group of teenaged boys to an arcade game, and found that all of them had unclean sexual thoughts. Of course, the researchers got the same result when they exposed the boys to coleslaw, an alpaca sweater, and "The MacNeil-Lehrer News Hour," but that is beside the point. The point is that we should all write letters to our elected officials and urge them to ban video games.

And while they're at it, they should also ban golf. Golf is similar to video games in that it is a monumentally useless activity that people become obsessed with and waste a lot of money on, but it has the added drawback of encouraging people to wear really stupid clothing, such as pants that can be seen with the naked eye from other galaxies. I strongly suspect that if our nation's youth continue to play video games, many of them will eventually graduate to golf, so I say let's kill two birds with one stone and ban them both.

Now I know what you're thinking. You're thinking, "How, in a free country such as this, can we ban video games and golf, yet continue to permit stamp collecting?" You're absolutely right, and I'm only sorry I didn't think of it myself. It would be hard to conceive of an activity more useless than stamp collecting, except maybe water-skiing or the Rose Bowl parade, so I suppose these things will have to be banned too, along with fraternal organizations, music, tropical fish, racquetball, and any activity whatsoever involving Ed McMahon. Also, anybody attempting to operate a beauty pageant should be shot without trial.

Of course, this is only a partial list of the useless, fiber-destroying activities that should be banned, and I'm sure you'll think of plenty more when you write to your elected officials. The important thing isn't so much *what* you want to ban; it's the fact that you participate in the banning process. That's what democracy is all about.

Subtract Those Ads

I STRONGLY SUSPECT that the people who appear in television commercials are imported from the planet Jupiter. I can think of no other way to explain their behavior. Take, for example, the commercials for Coca-Cola in which an extremely interracial group of people gathers on a hillside, holding candles, and sings:

> *I'd like to teach the world to sing*
> *In perfect har-mo-nee*
> *I'd like to buy the world a Coke*
> *And keep it com-pa-nee.*

This is not the way native Earth people behave. Native Earth people do not gather interracially on hillsides for any purpose other than to watch

98

motorcyclists leap over cars. And native Earth people, at least the ones I know, see no connection whatsoever between Coca-Cola and world harmony. In fact, I'm willing to bet statistics would show that Coca-Cola sales and world tension have both been increasing steadily for the past thirty years or so.

Now don't get me wrong. I am not saying Coca-Cola causes world tension. I happen to be very fond of Coca-Cola. It tastes fine, and it makes an excellent industrial cleanser. I'm just saying the people in Coca-Cola's commercials either are deranged or come from another planet.

And it's not just Coca-Cola commercials. You can watch commercials for days and never see anything approaching normal human behavior. I think that, in the interest of honesty, the government ought to pass a law requiring companies to use regular Earth people in their commercials. Here's how they would behave:

COMMERCIALS FOR MEN'S HAIR DARKENERS

(The commercial opens with a white-haired man and a dark-haired man standing in an office.)

WHITE-HAIRED MAN: I'm worried that the boss won't give me that Big Promotion.

DARK-HAIRED MAN: That's because you look too old. Here, take this hair-darkening stuff home and smear it in your hair every night.

WHITE-HAIRED MAN: Thanks a million. I'll try it.

(The scene shifts to the boss's office, several weeks later. The formerly white-haired man now has extremely dark, glossy hair. He looks as though he has a wet cat

on his head.)

BOSS: I called you in here to tell you I've decided to give you—My God, what's that on your head?

FORMERLY WHITE-HAIRED MAN: My hair. I've been smearing stuff on it every night.

BOSS: It looks like a wet cat.

FORMERLY WHITE-HAIRED MAN: What did you want to see me about?

BOSS: Uh, nothing. On your way out, ask my secretary to send in somebody who looks distinguished.

COMMERCIALS FOR HEADACHE
REMEDIES

(A woman is sitting at a table on which are four bottles. She is facing many bright lights. From behind the lights, a faceless man is talking to her.)

FACELESS MAN: Mrs. Jones do you have a headache?

WOMAN: Yes, and those lights aren't helping one bit.

FACELESS MAN: Which of these leading pain relievers do you think has the most laboratory-proven pain-killing ingredient?

WOMAN: You mean aspirin, right? Why do you guys always dream up these elaborate names for aspirin? Why don't you just call it aspirin? And why are you hiding behind those lights?

FACELESS MAN: Look, this leading brand has only 450 milligrams of laboratory-proven pain-killing ingredient. And this brand has only 450 milligrams. And this brand has only—

WOMAN: Shut up! Just shut up! Isn't it bad enough that I have a headache? Do I also have to sit here in front of a bunch of hot lights and listen to some idiot blither about milligrams? I'm going to go home and take some aspirin.

COMMERCIALS FOR SMOKER'S
TOOTH POLISH

(Two people are standing at a cocktail party, smoking cigarettes.)

FIRST SMOKER: Say, I have an idea: Why don't you exhale some cigarette smoke through this white handkerchief?

SECOND SMOKER: That sounds like a swell idea. *(He blows some smoke through the handkerchief.)*

FIRST SMOKER: Look at that brown glop. Imagine what that's doing to your teeth.

SECOND SMOKER: My *teeth?* What about my *lungs,* for God's sake? I've got to quit.

(The first smoker coughs violently and spits something disgusting into the handkerchief.)

COMMERCIALS FOR STOVE-TOP STUFFING

(A woman and her husband are shopping in a supermarket. A man with a microphone approaches them.)

MAN WITH MICROPHONE: Mrs. Brown, which do you think your husband would rather have for dinner: potatoes or Stove-Top Stuffing?

WOMAN: I don't see where that's any of your business.

MAN WITH MICROPHONE: Well, Mr. Brown?

HUSBAND: Geez, I don't know. Stove-Top Stuffing, I guess.

MAN WITH MICROPHONE: Well, Mrs. Brown, what do you think of that?

WOMAN: I think that if my husband is going to go around telling perfect strangers that he doesn't like the food I cook, then he can cook his own damn food.

COMMERCIALS FOR WISK LAUNDRY DETERGENT

(Two men are talking at a party, as their wives listen.)

FIRST MAN: I'm feeling really wrung out lately.

SECOND MAN *(jeeringly):* That's because you've got ring around the collar. Ha ha.

(The first man shakes his head sadly, then walks off.)

SECOND MAN: What's with him?

SECOND MAN'S WIFE: His mother just died, you idiot.

Low Finance

A Matter of Life and Debt

FIRST OF ALL, let me assure you that we are not in a depression. The key economic indicator of a depression is that you suddenly start seeing a lot of primitive black-and-white newsreel films of people wearing old-fashioned hats and overcoats and forming lines in the streets of major cities to obtain bread. So far, all the lines of people have been videotaped in color, which is the sign of a stable economy. Also, the people have not been lining up for bread. They have been lining up for cheese, which the government has several million tons of.

Some of you are no doubt wondering why the government has so much cheese. It's because of the Strategic Dairy Products Act, which was passed in 1947 to guarantee that the nation never becomes dependent on some unreliable foreign power, such as France, for its cheese supply. So for years the government has been paying huge sums of money to dairy farmers for cheese that winds up sitting in government warehouses as a permanent reminder to the cheese-making nations of the world that we are a strong, self-reliant people.

The problem is that after a few years the cheese hardens to the consistency of Formica, and the government has to get rid of it. The original plan, developed by Alexander Haig, was to drop the cheese from Air Force bombers onto rebel troops in El Salvador, but military analysts pointed out that the rebels might be able to melt it down and eat it, so the government decided instead to give it to poor people here in the United States. But this should not be taken as a sign that we are in a depression.

What we are in is a recession. The key economic indicator of a recession is that government economists go around announcing that the economy is improving. The truth, of course, is that government economists don't have the slightest notion what the economy is doing; if they did, they would have decent jobs. But they keep trying. Every few days they come out with some economic statistic and attempt to explain it, using charts and pointers, to the news media:

WASHINGTON—The U.S. Treasury's Bureau of Calculations announced today that the rate of increase of the Average Price of Things that People Buy So They Can Make Them into Other Things and Sell Them for More Money Than They Paid for Them was slightly lower than might otherwise have been expected. "This is a very, very hopeful sign," said government economist Elwood Welt, once he located the room where the press conference was held. "To be perfectly frank, we had feared that the rate of increase would be something like 6.67 percent, when in fact it was 6.53 percent, so we here at the Bureau of Calculations are extremely pleased and hopeful and will probably take the rest of the day off."

Government economists are always hopeful, for two reasons:

1. They have jobs.
2. If they aren't hopeful, the President will fire them.

So government economists go around with big smiles on their faces all the time. For the past thirty years, presidents increased spending and deficits like clockwork, and the government economists smiled. Then Ronald Reagan said he was against big spending and deficits, and the government economists smiled. Now it turns out that spending and deficits are still going up, and the government economists are still smiling. Phyllis George would be a good government economist.

The big question, of course, is, What can we, as citizens, do for the government during the recession? Well, for one thing, it would he a big help if we would stop being unemployed in such large numbers. A lot of us have managed to get ourselves unemployed lately, and some of us are guilty of extremely high interest rates. As a result, we are making it very difficult for government economists to remain hopeful. So far they have managed to pull it off, but it's only a matter of time before they start to feel depressed:

WASHINGTON—The U.S. Treasury's Bureau of Calculations announced today that the nation's economy is going to hell in a hand basket and probably will never get better: "I'm sorry, but I just can't feel hopeful about anything anymore," said government economist Elwood Welt, clutching a fifty-pound block of government surplus cheese. "We've tried everything. We've tried coming up with new statistics, we've tried using more colorful charts, and more recently we've tried drugs, but the truth is we are all very depressed about the economy and will probably take the rest of the day off."

Full-Service Bankruptcy

WHAT MAKES INTERNATIONAL FINANCE so fascinating is that, thanks to the miracle of modern electronic banking, you are linked financially with billions of people you don't even know, which means the actions of a deranged scum-bucket politician in some country you never even heard of could cause you to lose your home and your life's savings and wind up living in a cardboard refrigerator carton and licking discarded candy wrappers for nourishment. This has caused some people to be concerned about their banks. The banking industry has responded with reassuring television commercials, wherein a man wearing a reassuring suit says:

"We're the nation's banks, and we're not the least bit worried about anything, which is why we're spending hundreds of thousands of dollars to let you know that nobody is worried about anything. Here, for example, is an extremely solid bank. Just look at this momma." *(Here he kicks the bank.)* "You're talking solid masonry construction. And on top of that, your deposits are protected by the full faith and credit of the United States Government, the same organization that gave so many of you shots for swine flu. This means that if anything goes wrong with the banking system, your elected representatives will fly back from Switzerland or France or wherever they are, and they'll hold press conferences and call each other names, and eventually they're bound to come up with a nifty plan to get your money back. So there's nothing to worry about, nothing at all. Forget we even brought it up. Thank you."

To illustrate how you are connected to international finance, let's look at how the banking system works. First, people like yourself deposit money in banks. The banks put the money in their safes, where the amounts gradually increase thanks to the sound banking practice of never lending money to people like yourself. Eventually the bankers at the smaller banks get nervous about having all that money around, so they transfer it to gigantic international banks in New York, in return for which they receive very attractive desk calendars.

At this point, the gigantic international bankers are sitting around, wondering what to do with the money, when officials of a country such as Poland pull up in a taxi, race into the bank without paying the driver, and apply for a loan:

BANKERS: And just how much money did you have in mind?

POLISH OFFICIALS: We were thinking in terms of one million trillion dollars in small bills.

BANKERS: That's a great deal of money for us to lend to people who have horribly mismanaged their country's economy for years and whose authority depends on the armed oppression of the Soviet Union. What assurance do we have that you can repay us?

POLISH OFFICIALS: We're willing to sign our names to several pieces of paper.

BANKERS: Would tens and twenties be okay?

The Polish officials flee back to Poland with the money, all of which immediately disappears into the black market in exchange for Elton John records. After maybe five years, the international bank sends Poland a letter:

111

Dear Poland:

This is just a friendly note to remind you that, according to our records, you now have a past due balance of $832,674,709,908,772.54. Although we value you as a customer, continued tardiness in payment on your part could force us to precipitate an international banking crisis.

Warmest regards,
Your Gigantic Full-Service
International Bank

So the Poland officials telephone the bank collect and, shouting to be heard over the Elton John record playing in the background, claim the check is in the mail.

Over the years, this process has been repeated with so many countries that virtually all the money originally deposited in U.S. banks is now in the hands of foreign street vendors, which is why your local bank is willing to give you calculators and toasters if you'll deposit more money. This can't go on, of course. Already, some banks have taken drastic corrective action in the form of lending more money to foreign countries so they can make their interest payments. But this may not be enough; we may soon see a day when the United States Government, fed up with the incredible stupidity of the international bankers, finally steps in and gives them enormous amounts of money taken from taxpayers, which is only fair, because the taxpayers were the ones who got the toasters.

The Net May Be Gross

THE REASON THAT YOU ARE NOT extremely wealthy, of course, is that you do not carefully keep track of your finances. John D. Rockefeller carefully kept track of *his* finances, and he ended up with so much money that he started giving it away in bales, and many of his offspring became governors. For a while there, we barely had enough states for Rockefellers to be governors of. So if you want your offspring to be governors, you should drive down to your local office-supplies store and get yourself a little accountant-style notebook and immediately start writing down your expenses:

- Accountant-style Notebook—$7.97
- Gas Used to Get to Store for Accountant-Style Notebook—$1.14
- Depreciation on Car—$4.34
- Parking—$1.25
- Beef Jerky Purchased at Convenience Store on Way Home—$.99
- Damage to Fender Caused by Uninsured Motorist While Car Was in Convenience Store Parking Lot—$385.62
- Knife Wound Suffered in Argument—$1,830.88
- Legal Fees—$12,757.21

See? You're on your way to riches. Not only do you know exactly where your money is going, but all these items are tax-deductible, provided you were talking to your lawyer when you ate the beef jerky.

When you get home, you should sit down and try to figure out what your major assets are. There are two kinds of assets: "liquid" assets are the ones you have already spent, and "solid" assets are the ones you still have. In our household, our major asset is roughly $4,000 worth of pennies under the furniture. These pennies are a fairly solid asset, because to get them we would have to crawl around and stuff them into those little wrappers you get at the bank, and the bank probably wouldn't accept them anyway, because of the high floor-lint content. Our other major solid assets are:

- $42.13 worth of U.S. postage stamps that we bought only recently but cannot use because the Postal Commission raises the rate every two or three days.
- $3,024.56 worth of aquarium supplies, from when my wife and I went through our Tropical Fish Phase, which culminated in our discovery that they are called "tropical" fish because they can survive only in the tropics, which we do not live in.
- A purebred German shepherd dog for which we paid $300, or roughly $50 per brain cell.
- $80 worth of rolls of undeveloped photographic film, which we don't want to have developed because we can't remember whether they contain any memorable pictures, but which we don't want to throw away in case they contain any memorable pictures. We've had these rolls for years now, and we often take them off the shelf and settle down in front of a crackling fire to look at them and reminisce. "Remember this roll of film?" we say.
- $200 worth of random keys.

***

114

YOUR ONLY REMAINING financial responsibility is to balance your checkbook. Every month, you send out a batch of checks to various people, and every month the bank gets hold of these checks somehow, smears them with bank-style graffiti, and sends them back to you. The obvious question, of course, is, What are you supposed to do with them? My wife ignores them. She merely tosses the bank envelope, unopened, into a drawer, and walks away, laughing a carefree laugh. So far, she has gotten away with it, but I'm fairly sure that someday the Bank Inspector will show up with guns and attack dogs and make her stay in her room until she balances her checkbook. So I always balance mine. Here's the system I use:

> 1. On a large, flat surface, such as a washing machine or floor, arrange all the checks in a tasteful, numerical pattern.
> 2. With a sharp pencil, put little check marks next to all the numbers on the bank statement and all the numbers in your checkbook.

That's all there is to it. You could avoid even this much work if you could prevent the bank from getting hold of your checks and sending them back to you. One way to do this would be to write, in large letters at the top of each check, the words DO NOT LET THE BANK GET HOLD OF THIS CHECK. If everybody did this, we would all save thousands of hours we now waste balancing checkbooks, and we would probably have come up with a cure for the common cold by now.

Anti•Insurance Policy

I HAVE BEEN UNDER almost constant attack by life-insurance salesmen for most of my adult life. I was first attacked when I was in college, by this guy named Charlie. One day he was a normal college student, no different from the rest of us, and the next day he was a life-insurance salesman. It was as if the Moonies had got him. All of a sudden, he was wearing wing-tipped shoes and acting very concerned about my Financial Security. At the time, my idea of Financial Security was to have enough money to buy a pizza with extra cheese, but Charlie thought I should have at *least* six hundred thousand dollars' worth of life insurance, so that when I died my dependents would be rich.

To be honest, I didn't care what happened to my dependents, because I didn't have any. But Charlie was obsessed with my dependents: he'd sit in my room, hour after hour, and fret about them, until finally, to ease his mind, I bought some life insurance, and he went away. As soon as I was safely in another state, I cashed in my insurance and used the money to go sailing in the Virgin Islands with some friends who had not had the foresight to buy life insurance for their dependents, and thus had a more difficult time coming up with the money. So my life insurance turned out to be a good investment.

All life-insurance salesmen believe that no matter who you are, or what your financial situation is, you need more insurance. So unless you wear elaborate disguises and sleep in old refrigerator cartons, sooner or later a life-insurance salesman will come to your home, calling you by your first name a lot and subtly hinting that you're going to die. Suppose your name is John. Here's how your insurance salesman will attack you:

INSURANCE SALESMAN: John, I just stopped by to chat about your Financial Security. John, our records indicate that you're going to die someday and leave your dependents penniless and they'll end up out on the street eating garbage in the cold. I just thought we should chat about that, John.

YOU: Well, I certainly appreciate it, but I already have eight million dollars' worth of life insurance, and my only dependents are these tropical fish.

INSURANCE SALESMAN: Frankly, John, in these inflationary times, eight million dollars just isn't going to buy all that much tropical fish food. And I'm not even talking about the cost of fish-tank filters, John.

YOU: But they're just *fish,* for God's sake. I just can't see buying more insurance for fish. But thanks anyway.

INSURANCE SALESMAN: John, not long ago I was sitting in a room just like this, talking with a man, just like you, who thought he didn't need more insurance. I left his house, and the next day he was struck by lightning and run over by a bulldozer and his body was eaten by ants, and within a matter of days his fish had all developed fin rot, all because he didn't think he needed more insurance. So, John, if I were to leave your house tonight and something like that were to happen to you, I'd never forgive myself. So I'll just unroll my sleeping bag here and cook some freeze-dried food, of which I have a three-week supply, while you think about it, John. And another thing, John. John

117

John John John John.

***

FINALLY, OF COURSE, you will buy insurance. As the salesman leaves, he will put a secret mark on the door to alert other insurance salesmen that yours is a good house to stop at, and soon they will be at your door in droves. If you want them to go away, either you have to shoot them, which is illegal in some states and which doesn't always work anyway, or you have to buy more insurance.

So the only real solution to the problem is to convince the salesman that you are a bad risk. Put a sign outside your house that says CAUTION: RADIOACTIVE RABID LEPROSY VICTIM WITH SMALLPOX. This won't stop a really successful salesman from entering, but it will slow him down. When he knocks on the door, hide in the bedroom and have a friend, wearing a surgical mask, escort him into the living room. Then follow this script:

INSURANCE SALESMAN: Is John home?

YOUR FRIEND: Yes, but I think he's dead. Let me check. John? Are you dead?

YOU: Not yet. Who is it?

YOUR FRIEND: A visitor.

YOU: Oh, goody. Send him in. I haven't had a visitor since poor old Wesley Bumpers came to see me last week. Speaking of whom, I wish you'd get him out of here. He's beginning to spoil.

INSURANCE SALESMAN: Perhaps I've picked a bad time.

YOU: Not at all. Come on in. *(Here you cough violently, and toss a bucket of giblets into the living room.)*

118

INSURANCE SALESMAN: I just realized I'm late for an important appointment in Belgium. I'll stop by later. *(Holding his breath, he barges out the door.)*

If this approach doesn't work, you should try vicious dogs.

Build Your Own Mess

YOU YOUNG COUPLES out there who dream of having your own houses someday have probably read a lot of depressing articles about housing costs. You know:

WASHINGTON—The American Institute of People Who Keep Track of These Things released a study today showing that by 2010 the average single-family house will cost eleven million dollars, not counting drapes, and that the only people who will be able to afford houses will be members, of the Saudi Arabian royal family and major drug dealers.

Well, cheer up, young couples: you *can* have your own house. All you need is a large sum of money. The best source of money is your parents. You can get almost anything you want from your parents, provided you're not afraid to whine. I remember when I was twelve and really *needed* a BB gun. My parents didn't want me to have one, on the grounds I might shoot my brother. But I put together a string of about thirty-five days during which I was without question the most sniveling, obnoxious child in the entire world. It got to the point where, to preserve their sanity, my parents had to either give me a BB gun or hire someone to kidnap me. They eventually elected to buy me a BB

119

gun, mainly because it was cheaper. I was so grateful that I didn't shoot my brother for three or four days.

Anyway, your parents probably have a bunch of money rotting away in things like savings accounts and investments and pensions and insurance and retirement homes. So what you should do is follow your parents everywhere—to the supermarket, to work, to parties—tugging at their sleeves and saying "I wanna house." Sooner or later, because they love you, they'll give you some money. Or flee to Brazil.

If you can't get money from your parents, you may be able to get some from a bank. The trouble is that banks prefer to give money to people who already have a lot of it. If you walk into a bank looking like a poverty-stricken young couple whose own parents won't give them money, the loan officer will drum his fingers impatiently and try to get you out of his office so he can get back to increasing the prime rate. So you want to look wealthy. Wear tuxedos and evening gowns, and act as though you could not care less whether you get any money:

LOAN OFFICER: May I help you?

YOU: Yes. We'd like to grab a quick bite of pheasant while Jacques fuels the Mercedes. Could we have a table please?

LOAN OFFICER: I'm sorry, but this is a bank.

YOU: *A bank?* How very quaint. Is it for sale? I should think it would be *gobs* of fun to have a cozy little bank like this. Our others are so *huge.*

LOAN OFFICER: Uh, no, I'm afraid it's not for sale. But I could give you a loan. Would $300,000 do?

YOU: Thanks awfully, but we're all set for today.

LOAN OFFICER: How about $450,000? Please,

120

take it. We can sign the papers later.

If you can't get money from your parents or a bank, you can build your own house. Anybody can build a house. My father is a Presbyterian minister who knows only the basics of carpentry, and he built the house I grew up in. The only problems are that the house took him about thirty-five years to finish and in many ways looks like it was built by a Presbyterian minister who knows only the basics of carpentry. Also, some of the windows have BB-gun holes.

Here is how to build a house:

1. Find some land. You can find empty land all over the place, particularly along interstate highways. Pick out a nice batch of land and watch it for a few days: if nobody seems to be doing anything with it, you can assume it's okay for you to build a house there.

2. Dig a ditch in the shape of the house. If you run into a lot of rocks and stuff, forget the ditch. You're going to put a house on top of it anyway, so nobody will know the difference.

3. Get several thousand boards at a lumberyard and nail them together so they form a house. (NOTE: Do *not* do this at the lumberyard.)

If you don't want to go to all this trouble, you can just put up a crude but made of animal skins or mud and twigs. No matter what you build, you'll be able to sell it for hundreds of thousands of dollars in a few years, when you need the money to get your children to stop following you around saying "I wanna house."

God Needs the Money

HERE ARE THREE TYPES of people you should not trust:

• *People who tell you God told Them to tell you to send them money.* You know the guys I mean. They get on television and say: "God told me He wants you to send me some money, say $100, or even just $10, if that's all you can afford, but in all honesty I must point out that God is less likely to give you some horrible disease if your gift is in the $100 range."

The theory here seems to be that God talks only to the guys on television. I always thought that if God needed money all that badly, He would get in touch with us directly.

My wife gets a lot of letters from people who say God told them to tell her to send them money. She got a great one recently from Brother Leroy Jenkins, who is evidently one of the people God goes to when He needs a *lot* of money. Leroy is very straightforward:

The Lord spoke to me to have you send a onetime large gift. Will you send me $1,000, or $500, or $100, or even $5,000? . . . If you are not able to send all of the $1,000, $500, $100, or $5,000 now, send as much as you can, and make a vow to the Lord that you will send an offering of $20 (or at least $10) each month.

Notice you make the vow to the *Lord,* but you send the money to *Leroy.* Leroy doesn't specify what he plans to do with it, but he does tell you to send it to him at the Walden Correctional Institution in South Carolina, where he is serving a twelve-year term for criminal conspiracy. I imagine God advised him to get a good lawyer.

• *People who say they want to do things for the Public.* I have yet to locate the Public: all I ever see is people. Nevertheless, some people are *certain* there's a Public out there somewhere, sort of like the Lost Continent of Atlantis, and they keep trying to *do* things for it. Generally, these things consist of taking money away from people to help the Public, or passing laws prohibiting people from doing things that most people see nothing wrong with, but that are not in the Public Interest. For example:

—The federal government helps the Public by taking ever larger amounts of money away from most people. The theory is that if the government didn't step in, people would spend the money on things they want, which would cause inflation, which would be bad for the Public. So the government takes the money and (surprise!) spends it.

—Most states protect the Public by limiting people to only one telephone company, electric company, and so on. This is Good for the Public. It is not to be confused with monopolies, which are Bad for the Public.

—Your really enlightened states protect the Public by prohibiting everybody but the state from operating liquor or gambling businesses. These businesses are considered Bad if people operate them, but Good if the state does, even though the only real difference is that state liquor stores have high prices, poor selection, and all the charm of unwashed junior high school locker rooms; and state gambling games offer sucker odds and idiot advertisements that appeal most to people who can least afford to throw money away.

123

I want to clarify one point: When I talk about "people," I am not talking about "the People" with a capital "P" as in "Power to the People" and other such slogans, which are bandied about by people who really mean "Power to Me and a Few of My Friends Who Know What Is Good for the People." Generally, these people merely want to get control over property that is already owned by people, only not the right ones.

• *People who say they are doing things in Your Interest.* Don't trust anybody who says he's doing something in Your Interest, except maybe your mother. Let's face it: most people do what they do because they enjoy it or make money from it, and there's nothing wrong with that. But most people feel obligated to pretend all they ever think about is helping the human race, especially you. Life-insurance salesmen, for example, tend to carry on as though the only reason they sell life insurance is that they feel it is more beneficial than the priesthood. Advertisements work the same way. The Chrysler Corporation wants me to buy a Chrysler not because it sells Chryslers, but because it wants to Help America. Mobil isn't trying to sell petroleum products: it's trying to Solve the Energy Crisis. And so on.

SO THERE YOU HAVE IT: a list of people not to trust. You should be grateful you have someone like me, working for the Public Good, with Your Interest in mind. God wants you to send me some money.

Health Habits

Exercising Your Rights

LET'S TALK ABOUT exercise and your body. First, the bad news. You cannot have a really swell body, like the one belonging to Victoria Principal. Victoria is the actress from the famous television show "Dallas" who appears in newspaper and television advertisements wearing a stretch garment that, if not occupied by Victoria Principal, would contract to the size of a gum wrapper.

In the television commercial, Victoria walks around a health club striking various bodily poses and saying something. You can't hear what she's saying, because when you see this particular commercial your brain tends to devote all available nervous-system resources to your eyes, but the gist of it is that if you join a health club and exercise a lot you will look like Victoria Principal or one of the major hunks of manhood behind her.

This is a lie, of course. Mother Nature, in her infinite wisdom, has decided that only a select few people can look like Victoria Principal or the hunks, and you are not one of them. These select people are destined to have swell bodies even if the only exercise they get is eating Slim Jims and drinking cheap whiskey. Certain other people can exercise constantly and eat nothing but grapefruit rinds, but they will still have the bodies of water buffalo.

This is probably for the best. Think how dull the world would be if we did not have wide variations in our bodily formats. We'd be like ants. If you've ever taken a good, close look at a batch of ants, you've probably noticed that they're all equally attractive. You never see any fat ants, or buxom ants, or lean, sinewy ants. They all have identical, perfect little ant bodies, and consequently they find each other boring. Put yourself in their position: how would you feel if you lived in a world where every member of the opposite sex had a perfect body? You'd crave something different. You'd start casting a speculative glance toward the larvae, or even the pupae. If you were a male ant, you might even make a pass at, say, a queen termite, despite the fact that she is about sixty times your size, lays thirty-five thousand eggs a day, and tends to devour her sexual partners. Or is that spiders? No matter. The mere fact that you would even consider making a pass at a termite is proof of my point, which, i£ I recall it correctly, is that Mother Nature wants us all to be different, which means that if you are basically a squat person, you can exercise all you want, and you will still be basically a squat person.

This does not mean you shouldn't exercise; it merely means that you should understand the *real* reason you should exercise, which is to prepare your body for the pain you'll inevitably have to endure when you become older. Let's say you're in your mid-twenties to mid-thirties. Most of the time you feel pretty good, right? The only time you feel really lousy is when you attend a major party and ingest huge quantities of alcohol and wake up the next day naked in an unfamiliar city. But as you grow older, you're going to start feeling more aches and pains caused by the inevitable afflictions of age, such as arthritis, the Social Security Administration, condescending denture-adhesive commercials, children who call only when they want to borrow money for down payments on houses much nicer than the one you live in, et cetera. You need to prepare your body for this pain. This is why exercise is so important.

Take joggers. You see them running along the street, clearly hating every second of it, and you say, "What's the point?" Ha. Years from now, you'll struggle to adjust to the aches and pains of growing older, whereas the joggers, who have been in constant agony for fifteen or twenty years, will be able to make the transition smoothly, unless they've committed suicide.

So don't delay. Start an exercise program today, the more painful the better. If you don't like to jog, buy the exercise book that Jane Fonda, the noted critic of capitalism, sells for $17.95, and do the exercises in it. Or just hit yourself repeatedly in the head with it.

Programs for the Unfit

OKAY! TODAY'S THE DAY you start on your physical-fitness program, the program that's going to make you slender, healthy, and attractive, like the people in cigarette advertisements.

Step one is to take your pulse, because a healthy heart is the key to physical fitness. If your heart is healthy, you can continue to collect Social Security long after your other major organs have become senile and are wandering around aimlessly with no idea what bodily functions they are supposed to perform. The best way to understand the relationship between your heart and your health is to examine an actual heart. You cannot, of course, examine your own heart, unless you have a high threshold of pain, so instead you should trot down to the grocery store and ask the butcher for some surplus hearts from an assortment of animals—a cow, a pig, a fish, an earthworm, et cetera. Most butchers will be happy to give you the hearts for free, just to get you to go away.

Now take your hearts home, spread them out on a clean, level surface, such as a Ping-Pong table, and examine them closely. You'll notice that the hearts differ in size, but they have one important thing in common: *the animals they were removed from are all dead.* This tells us that hearts are extremely important for physical fitness. Now place your hearts in Tupperware containers and store them in your freezer in case your children ever need them for science-fair projects or practical jokes.

Now you're ready to take your pulse. The traditional method is to locate the major artery that goes through your wrist and press your thumb against it. The only potential drawback to this method is that you might squash the artery flat with your thumb, causing the blood to back up so that eventually your arm explodes like a party balloon. A safer way is to drink gin and tonic until you can actually hear your pulse pounding in your head, then walk or crawl to a nearby store and tell the salesperson you want to buy a stopwatch so you can count the number of pounds per minute:

YOU: I want a stopwatch.

SALESPERSON: We don't sell stopwatches. This is a grocery store.

YOU *(picking up an eggplant):* Oh yeah? Then what do you call this?

SALESPERSON: That's an eggplant. Say, you're the guy who was in here earlier asking for fish hearts. Are you drunk or something?

YOU: Certainly not. As any idiot can plainly see,

I'm taking my pulse.

SALESPERSON: With an eggplant? Why don't you just squash your thumb against your artery like everybody else?

YOU *(with great dignity)*: If I wanted a squash, I would have selected a squash, wouldn't I? I'll take this eggplant, and make it snappy.

NEXT, USING A STOPWATCH or an eggplant, count the number of times your head pounds in a minute; if you're a healthy person, this should be a two- or three-digit number. Now you're ready to start your exercise program. Turn on your television and watch one of those programs in which people in skimpy outfits leap around in time to recorded music under the direction of a cheerful leader.

Notice I say you should *watch* the program: under no circumstances should you actually *do* the exercises, because all that leaping around will reduce your brain to tapioca pudding. You'll wind up like the people on the television programs, smiling vacantly and doing whatever the cheerful leader tells you to:

LEADER: Okay! Let's kick those legs up high! Great! Now let's bend way over! Terrific! Now let's all say "I pledge allegiance to the Reverend Sun Myung Moon."

EXERCISERS: I pledge allegiance to the Reverend Sun Myung Moon.

LEADER: Okay! Now let's all hop on one foot and put our fingers in our noses! Great! Now let's all take out our checkbooks and. . .

AFTER YOUR EXERCISE PROGRAM, take your pulse again, then go to the kitchen and prepare a large, nutritious breakfast. You may not feel hungry, especially after all the pulse taking, so to boost your appetite, think about how important good nutrition is to your heart. Think about what will happen to you if you don't take good care of your heart. Think, as you chew your food, about what happened to the cow, the pig, the fish, and the earthworm whose hearts are sitting in Tupperware containers only a few feet away from your breakfast, sheathed in frozen slime. This should give you all the incentive you need to eat a hearty breakfast, after which you'll be ready to face the day or go back to bed.

Jogging for President

LATELY, I have noticed large numbers of people staggering along the sides of major highways, trying to get in shape. I think they have the right idea: most of us Americans are out of shape. I know for a fact that I am.

When I was in high school, my friends and I were in terrific shape. Our bodies were fine-tuned machines. We would routinely drink quarts of warmish beer, then perform feats of great physical prowess. For example, during the Halloween Dance we carried a 1962 Volkswagen all the way up the front steps of Pleasantville High School, right into the lobby. I bet we couldn't do that today. I bet you couldn't, either.

Now I grant you that most of us no longer feel any great *need* to drink warm beer and carry Volkswagens into high schools, but the point is that if some emergency arose, if for some reason involving national security we *had* to carry a Volkswagen into a high school, we couldn't do it. We'd go a few steps, then we'd drop the Volkswagen and collapse on the ground, gasping and heaving, and that would be the end of our national security. So I figure it's time to get in shape.

But jogging is not the way to do it. For one thing, jogging kills your brain cells. The Army has known this for years; it forces recruits to jog every day, on the theory that some of them will lose so many brain cells that they will eventually reenlist. Your really dedicated joggers know it, too; in fact, it's one of the main reasons they jog. The idea is that if you're troubled about your job or world affairs, you go out and jog until you've killed whatever brain cells are responsible for those thoughts. The problem is that you may also kill the brain cells that remember your name and address, in which case you keep right on jogging, sometimes for days. This is what has happened to the people you see jogging along major highways, the ones with vacant expressions on their faces: they left home as nuclear physicists, heart surgeons, corporation presidents, and so on, but after a few hours most of them have library paste for brains.

Remember Jimmy Carter? Every day at the White House he used to wake up at the crack of dawn, develop some brilliant plan to save the economy, then head out for his morning jog. His aides would find him stumbling around hours later, sweaty and confused, his economic plan gone forever. Jimmy might have stood a chance in the 1980 elections if he had run against another jogger, but instead he faced Ronald Reagan. Ron has his horses jog for him and thus is able to preserve what brain cells he has, although I suspect his horses are fairly stupid.

My other objection to jogging is that even if you manage to jog yourself into shape, you still don't *look* all that great. I mean, look at marathon runners: they appear gaunt and desperately hungry, like refugees wearing numbers. They're always snatching scraps of food from spectators and stuffing them (the scraps of food) into their mouths. If you were to toss, say, a side of raw beef into their path, they'd all dive for it, teeth bared, and that would be the end of the marathon.

So I have rejected jogging as a way to get in shape. In fact, I was about to give up altogether when I discovered body-building magazines. Body-building magazines are published for people, mostly male, whose idea of being in shape is to have muscles the size of lawn tractors. You've probably seen these magazines: they're full of pictures of people who have smeared Vaseline all over their bodies and are wearing bathing suits no larger than a child's watchband; they are trying to smile in a relaxed manner but end up with more of an intense grin, because they have enormous muscles lunging out from all over their bodies, and Lord only knows how many bizarre chemical substances coursing through their veins.

These people obviously do not jog—I doubt they ever leave their gymnasiums, for fear their muscles will lunge out and kill innocent bystanders—but they are obviously in *terrific* shape. At least they *look* as if they're in terrific shape, which is the important thing. If Jimmy Carter had spent his time body-building instead of jogging, he would be president today. His aides would have carried him into the presidential debates and propped him up against his lectern, and when it was time for him to make his opening statement, he would have just stood there, Vaseline shimmering on his muscles, grinning intensely at the audience. Who would have dared to vote against him?

134

So I've been reading body-building magazines, hoping to pick up some tips on getting in shape. The idea seems to be to lift a lot of heavy objects until you get dense. Density is much sought after in the body-building world. For example, *Muscle Digest* magazine, in its October issue, refers to one promising body-builder as "one of the most dense body-builders in senior level competition." Evidently this is considered high praise.

So I plan to lift heavy objects, starting with my typewriter and working up to a 1962 Volkswagen, until I get fairly dense, after which I intend to smear Vaseline on my body and maybe run for president.

A Cold Cure? Who Nose?

I SAY we give the medical community two more weeks to cure the common cold, and, if it doesn't, we turn over the problem to a more competent outfit, like the Sony Corporation. Sometimes I wonder what the medical community is thinking. We give it *bundles* of money to buy office furniture and white coats and other medical devices, and all it seems to want to do is invent obscure new operations nobody you know or I know ever needs:

CHICAGO—A team of surgeons at the Warpfinger Medical Institute here had successfully implanted a tiny electronic device into the right tonsil of a fifteen-year-old boy. "We don't really know why we did it," said a spokesman. "We just had this tiny electronic device and this fifteen-year-old boy, so we figured, why not? Next week we're going to install the battery."

Meanwhile, millions of people are out here getting

135

common colds and generally making the world a tackier place to live in. You have two kinds of cold victims: your nose blowers and your snorters. For overall ability to make you want to walk out of restaurants, I'd have to give the edge to the nose blowers. And they are everywhere. Americans think nothing of public nose blowing. They *encourage* it in their young. My fourth-grade teacher once spent *two hours* instructing us on nose blowing. She never married.

As far as I can tell, the only groups trying to do anything useful about the common cold are the cold-remedy companies that advertise on TV:

(The scene opens in a pleasant suburban home. The husband walks in through the front door and speaks to his wife who is wearing a bathrobe and lying on the floor.)

HUSBAND: Are you ready to go visit my father at the Home for Sickly Old People?

WIFE: I don't think I can, dear. It's this darn cold. I have a fever of 112 degrees and I can no longer move anything on the left side of my body.

HUSBAND: Here, try some Phlegm-B-Gone.

WIFE: Phlegm-B-Gone?

HUSBAND: Phlegm-B-Gone.

(The scene shifts to an impressive office with a big desk. On a shelf behind the desk is a huge collection of books. It is actually the complete series, but the camera doesn't get close enough for you to realize this. A medical-looking actor, wearing a white coat, is standing in front of the desk, holding a clipboard.)

MEDICAL-LOOKING ACTOR: Medical tests show that Phlegm-B-Gone, a collection of medical ingredients, is extremely medical when used in a conscientiously applied program of oral hygiene and regular professional care. Get back on your feet with Phlegm-B-Gone.

(The scene shifts to the Home for Sickly Old People.)

WIFE: Gosh, that Phlegm-B-Gone, with a collection of medical ingredients, is great! I'm back on my feet again with only a slight limp!

HUSBAND: I'm beginning to feel a little feverish. How about you, Dad? . . . Dad? . . . Dad?

SOME PEOPLE THINK the way to avoid colds is to eat a lot of vitamin C, something on the order of nine billion pentagrams a day. My wife believes in this approach. She's always choking down vitamin C pills, which are the size of toaster ovens. She gets colds anyway. My approach is to drink large quantities of beer. It seems to work. Since I started drinking large quantities of beer, I have not had one cold that I remember clearly.

Male Delivery Room

NOTE—If you are a little kid, and your parents have not yet told you about sex and where babies come from, do NOT read this column, because it contains a lot of stuff you would *kill* to find out.

THINGS GO IN AND OUT OF FASHION. Take water. For years, water was unfashionable, something to wash bird droppings off the car with. Today, water is fashionable, something to be advertised on national television by great men such as Orson Welles. (I use "great" not in the sense of "superior," but in the sense of "considerably larger than Zanesville, Ohio.") So today you'll see people paying $2.50 and more for fancy-looking six-packs of water. Five years ago, these people would have been considered stupid. Today, they are considered fashionable. Stupid, but fashionable.

Another example is babies. They were out of fashion during the seventies. Young couples were too busy. They'd say: "Should we have a baby? Should we embark on this great human adventure, which brings with it great responsibility, but also great joy and fulfillment? Nah, let's play tennis."

But babies are back in fashion. In the past year or two, many a couple has decided to sacrifice material things for the chance to create a new life, a life capable of love and hate, a life capable of dreams and desires, a life capable of excreting things in large volumes from three or four orifices at the same time.

But before *you* decide to have a baby, let me warn you, particularly you males:

They have changed the rules.

When your parents had you, the responsibilities of childbirth were clearly defined:

• THE WOMAN went to the doctor regularly, read a lot about pregnancy, made sure she ate the right foods, kept track of the baby's growth inside her, bought baby clothes and furniture, told the doctor when contractions began, timed them, made sure she got to the hospital on time, went to the delivery room, went through labor, and had the baby.
• THE MAN smoked cigarettes.

This system is obviously fair, and it worked well for

138

years. But somewhere along the line, some sinister granola-oriented group got to the medical community and the women's magazines and convinced them that *the man should become more involved.* That's right, men: they want you *right there in the delivery room when it happens.* Not only that, they want you to go to classes at which people *openly discuss pregnancy.*

I found all this out the hard way.

Let me assure you that I want to play a responsible role in my wife's pregnancy. I am willing to pace for *hours* in the waiting room with the other fathers-to-be and old copies of *National Geographic.* I am willing to go to classes on how to pace in the waiting room. But at our classes we don't talk about pacing: we talk about *what goes on inside a pregnant person's body.* I don't want to *know* what goes on inside my *own* body. I think if the Good Lord had wanted us to know what goes on inside our bodies, He would have given us little windows.

Another thing we do at our classes is practice breathing. That's right: *breathing.* The idea is the man helps the woman breathe steadily and imagine she's on a beach; this takes her mind off her labor and helps her relax. They haven't told us men how *we're* supposed to relax. I can see it now: my wife will be breathing steadily, imagining she's on a beach; I will be breathing shallowly, imagining I am lying on the delivery-room floor, because I *am* lying on the delivery-room floor.

I could go on: I could tell you about how the women in the class talk about really *personal* things in hearty, cheerful tones while we males stare intently at various ceiling tiles. But you'll find out anyway, if you haven't already.

At our last class, the leader said we're going to see a

139

film soon. I just *know* my wife will have to drive us home afterward.

Tale of the Tapeworm

THE HUMAN BODY is an amazing machine. Mine is, anyway. For example, I regularly feed my body truly absurd foods, such as Cheez Doodles, and somehow it turns them into useful bodily parts, such as glands. At least I *assume* it turns them into useful bodily parts; otherwise, there must be a huge wad of Cheez Doodles hidden away in my body somewhere, and eventually it will have to be removed in a major and fairly disgusting operation.

I learned about the human body in high school biology class, which covered everything except sex. Sex was covered in health class, which mainly involved how many different kinds of venereal disease there are (fourteen million); how high school students get venereal disease (merely by holding hands firmly); and whether it is a good idea for high school students to get venereal disease (no). These days, of course, high school students learn about the more positive aspects of sex, which is why so many of them have vacant smiles.

In biology, we learned about all the different systems of the body, mainly so we could find out how many things could go wrong with them. My biology teacher would describe, in loving detail, the many diseases we could get, and we students would imagine we were getting them. I went home with a new disease every night.

I was particularly susceptible to parasitic worms. The teacher was always telling us about these little worms that were trying to get into our bodies, often disguised as pieces of pork, so they could be parasites. We spent several classes on tapeworms, which get into your intestines. When I was writing this column, I decided to brush up on tapeworms (we should all brush up on tapeworms from time to time), so I looked them up in the *Encyclopaedia Britannica,* which says:

"Tapeworms . . . occur worldwide and range in size from about one millimeter (0.04 inch) to more than 15 meters (50 feet) . . ."

Think of that. Assuming you are a person of average height, at this very moment you could contain a worm nearly *ten times as long as you are*. If you suspect that you *do* contain a fifty-foot tapeworm, I advise you to feed it raw pork or whatever else it wants. Do *not* try to get it out, or anger it in any way; we have enough trouble in the world without huge, angry parasitic worms thrashing about.

If anything besides tapeworms goes wrong with your body, you should get a large quantity of money and go to a doctor. Everybody is always picking on doctors just because they charge high fees and rarely cure anything, but this is unfair. I mean, look at it from the *doctors'* point of view: they are healthy, intelligent people who spend years in medical schools, dealing with lots of other healthy, intelligent people; then they have to go out and deal with members of the *public,* most of whom are sick and have no medical training. As far as doctors are concerned, the worst part about practicing medicine is having to deal with sick, untrained people all the time. Some doctors solve this problem by becoming surgeons, who wear masks and deal only with patients who are unconscious and strapped down. Others become specialists, who issue opinions from motor yachts and never see patients at all.

But most doctors are stuck in offices, and eventually they have to see actual conscious patients. What is worse, these patients generally insist on trying to explain their medical problems. Doctors *hate* this. I mean, they didn't spend all those hours learning such things as where the pyloric valve is located just so they could listen to some idiot *patient* talk about medicine. So most doctors follow this rule: *The patient is always wrong.* This is why most doctor-patient conversations go like this:

PATIENT: I broke my leg.

DOCTOR: What makes you say that?

PATIENT: A tree fell on me and my leg went "snap." Look, a jagged piece of bone is sticking out of my thigh.

DOCTOR: The symptom you describe could well be caused by a dysfunction of the endocrinological system.

PATIENT: But my leg—

DOCTOR: I'm going to schedule you for a series of tests at the Mayo Clinic next month, and in the meanwhile, I'll consult with several specialists by marine radio. I suggest you avoid fatty foods.

So if you know what's wrong with you, your best bet is to tell your doctor you think something else is wrong with you. That way you stand some chance of actually getting treated.

Injurious to Your Wealth

I UNDERSTAND "M*A*S*H" is going off the air,which means I will have to get a new doctor. For the past few years, I have been telling my life-insurance agent that my doctor is Alan Alda. My agent needs to know who my doctor is so he can increase my life-insurance coverage, which he does roughly every couple of months. He'll call me up and say, "Dave, I've been reviewing your files, and I really think we need to increase your coverage, now that you have a child." And I'll say, "But, Jeff, we had the child two years ago, and we have used that excuse to increase my coverage four times since then." And he'll say, "Oh yeah, right. But I still think we ought to increase your coverage, because, ummmm, the cost of living has been going up." And I'll say, "It sure has, Jeff, especially the cost of my life-insurance premiums." And he'll say, "That's exactly the kind of thing I'm talking about, Dave. Think how difficult it would be for your wife to pay your life-insurance premiums if God forbid you were dead."

This goes on for a half hour or so, until finally I agree to increase my coverage because otherwise I won't be able to get off the phone and earn enough money to pay my premiums. Then Jeff says, "All I need, Dave, is the name of your doctor." I don't know why life-insurance companies always want the name of your doctor. Maybe they use it to check your credit rating. Or maybe they have a master list of really incompetent doctors, doctors whose patients come in with minor ear infections and wind up getting open-heart surgery, and if you have one of these doctors your premiums are adjusted upward. All I know is that Jeff won't get off the phone until I name a doctor.

I used to give him the name of the doctor who gave me my physical examinations for my life-insurance application. He was a terrific doctor, because he specialized in insurance examinations, which means he was not the least bit interested in the internal workings of my body. All he was interested in was filling out the insurance application, which is a long list of questions, sort of like the college-entrance examinations, except that the correct answer is always no. If you answer yes, you run the risk that you won't be allowed to pay the premiums, so the doctor reads the questions very quickly and checks "no" before you get a chance to answer:

DOCTOR: Have you or any member of your family or anybody you played with as a child ever had any funny tingling sensations?

YOU: Well, I—

DOCTOR *(checking "no")*: Have you ever sat bolt upright in bed in the middle of the night with a sharp pain in your abdomen and thought it might be appendicitis but couldn't remember whether your appendix is on the right or the left side so you woke up your spouse and he or she was somewhat irritable?

YOU: Well, once—

DOCTOR: *(checking "no")*: What about endotoxic infections? Salmonella typhosa? Acne? Clostridium botulinum? Semicolons? Ricketts? Tired blood? What is the capital of Idaho?

YOU: Would you remind repeating—

DOCTOR: *(checking "no")*: Okay. Now cough.

I liked this approach, because I never had to spend more than ten minutes with the insurance doctor, and he never tried to inject any foreign substances into my body. So I always said he was my doctor, until he retired, which is when I switched to Alan Alda.

I picked Alan Alda because he is a peck of fun. This is because he is in the Korean War, which, as you

144

know if you watch "M*A*S*H," is a zany, wacky, fun war, so much fun that it has been going for ten years now. I always figured that if I got sick, I could be flown directly to Korea, where Alan Alda would heal me within a half hour and introduce me to one of the several dozen attractive nurses who work in the M*A*S*H unit, and we could all go off and drink martinis and talk about how awful war is and then make lots of hilarious remarks, except for the nurses, who never say anything because their job is to mop Alan Alda's brow.

But "M*A*S*H" is going off the air, so I need a new doctor. I'm seriously considering Robert Young, who stunned the medical world a few years back when he discovered that virtually all major psychological disorders can be cured through the regular use of caffeine-free coffee.

Psychiatrist for Rent

PSYCHIATRY HAS GOTTEN a lot of attention ever since the court case in which John W Hinckley, Jr., was charged with being sane. Those of you who do not understand our legal system probably thought Hinckley had been charged with shooting the President and several other people, because that is what he did. But everybody knew he had done it, so the trial would have been fairly short:

DEFENSE ATTORNEY: My client, John W. Hinckley, Jr.—
JURY: Guilty.

So to put some meat on the trial, the judge decided

that the prosecution would have to prove that Hinckley was sane. Apparently, being sane is now a federal offense. As a result, the lawyers pretty much ignored the actual shootings, which everybody had seen on television anyway, and instead spent the bulk of the trial showing the movie *Taxi Driver* and getting testimony from rented psychiatrists, who explained that Hinckley clearly was or was not insane, depending on which psychiatrist happened to be on the witness stand:

PROSECUTING ATTORNEY: So, Dr. Warble, would you say that the defendant is sane?

PSYCHIATRIST: Oh yes indeed, very sane. Extremely sane.

DEFENSE ATTORNEY: I object, Your Honor. The defense rented this psychiatrist, and he is supposed to say that the defendant is insane.

PSYCHIATRIST: Oh yeah, that's right. What I mean is the defendant is *in*sane. Sorry.

The defense psychiatrists proved beyond a shadow of a doubt that Hinckley shot the President because he (Hinckley) was in love with Jodie Foster and had watched *Taxi Driver* many times, so he was acquitted. This makes sense to me. I think we can all agree that anyone who fell in love with Jodie Foster and watched *Taxi Driver* many times would have no option but to shoot the President. I think Hinckley should be set free, and Congress should pass a law requiring Miss Foster to date him.

The only flaw in the Hinckley trial is that it left a lot of people with the impression that psychiatrists are just a bunch of bearded voodoo doctors who espouse confusing and wildly contradictory theories that have nothing to do with common sense. This is totally unfair. Many psychiatrists are clean-shaven.

146

To understand why psychiatrists behave as they do, you have to understand the history of their profession. In primitive times, people believed that psychiatric disorders were caused by demons who possessed people, and primitive psychiatrists cured them by gouging holes in their skulls so the demons could get out (I am not making this up). Now, of course, we know that this is silly. The modern approach for getting rid of a demon is to have a priest dive out a fourth-floor window, as you know if you saw the fine documentary movie *The Exorcist,* which I imagine John Hinckley saw thirty-five times.

The other big cause of psychiatric disorders, besides demons, is your father. The man who discovered that fathers cause virtually all psychiatric problems was Sigmund Freud, who is known as the Father of Modern Psychiatry. Freud also discovered that if a trained analyst probed a patient's past for several hours a week, week after week, year after year, the analyst could make an enormous amount of money. Of course, the analyst must be very skilled, because otherwise the patient might go off on all kinds of irrelevant tangents unrelated to the father:

PSYCHIATRIST: And what seems to be the trouble?

PATIENT: I've been having these horrible, splitting headaches.

PSYCHIATRIST: And when did these headaches begin? Around the time you realized your father was a horrible man?

PATIENT: No, my father was a wonderful man. My headaches began last week, when I was working under my car and the jack broke and the car fell on my head.

I've also been bleeding from my ears.

PSYCHIATRIST: I see. And was your father's name Jack?

***

And so it goes, for a decade or so, until the patient realizes that his head aches because forty-seven years earlier his father wouldn't buy him an ice-cream cone.

Freud's approach is based on the fact that the human personality is actually made up of a number of parts: the Ego, the Libretto, the Sense of Humor, and the Tendency to Be Irritable in the Morning. The Libretto is trapped in the subconscious with nothing to read and consequently thinks about sex all the time. This embarrasses the other parts, so they clean up the thoughts before you actually get to think them. For example, let's say the Libretto thinks about a sexual organ. By the time you get it, the other personality parts have turned it into an aquarium, so that's what you *think* you're thinking about, you naïve fool. What this means is that everybody is actually thinking about sex all the time, although this becomes obvious only under intensive psychoanalysis or at office parties.

Freud's brilliant pioneering paved the way for new discoveries by future generations of psychiatrists, all of whom disagree with him and each other. We can only regret that Freud did not live to see his theories come to fruition, and maybe watch *Taxi Driver* a few times.

Oaf of Hippocrates

NOTE: BEFORE YOU READ this article about medical care, let me warn you that I am not a doctor. I did, however, study First Aid when I was in the Boy Scouts.

We scouts used to meet in the Methodist Church basement and apply tourniquets to each other, and we got really good at it. We once applied a tourniquet to Randy Lape that was so elaborate he couldn't move any part of his body, and he probably would have lain there until he starved to death if the choir hadn't shown up for rehearsal.

I have forgotten my First Aid training, except for one rule: When you encounter an injured person, you're not supposed to move him. At least I think that's the rule. Maybe the rule is that you're not even supposed to touch him. Maybe you're supposed to run away. Frankly, it's all a blur in my mind, along with the Morse Code, which is the other thing I learned in Boy Scouts, God only knows why.

Anyway, I just thought you should be aware of this before you read this article, assuming you still want to.

YOU SHOULD GET a thorough physical examination at least twice a year, unless you have to pay for it personally, in which case you should get one every eight years or whenever you think something is really wrong with you, whichever comes first.

You can usually tell when something is really wrong with you, because you feel really lousy even when you haven't been drinking. Sometimes you can cure yourself merely by calling your employer and saying, in a sincere, sick voice, that you won't be coming into work. If you have faked illnesses in the past, you should subtly let your employer know that you really are sick this time. Retch frequently, and say something like "I'm really sick this time. Really. *(Pause here for a retch.)* Honestly."

If you still feel lousy, you should identify your

symptoms and try to figure out exactly what's causing them. Here are the most popular symptoms:

• *Sharp, stabbing pains in the chest or stomach*—These are usually caused by being stabbed in the chest or stomach with a sharp object, but it could be something worse.

• *Dull, aching pains in the head*—These are usually caused by a headache. Often, you can cure yourself merely by being irritable; if that doesn't work, you may need aspirin or brain surgery.

• *Vomiting*—This is usually caused by eating clams.

If your symptoms don't go away, you should call your doctor's office. Notice I say "doctor's office," not "doctor." Under American Medical Association rules, doctors are not allowed to talk to patients over the telephone, because this would be unethical.

So when you call the doctor's office, you will talk to a medical personnel wearing a white outfit, whose job is to make an appointment for you to come in roughly six weeks later. If you are really sick, and you are a regular patient, the medical personnel may agree to talk to the doctor on your behalf, and your doctor may agree to phone the drugstore and order you a little bottle of pills that costs $34.38. But if you are really *really* sick, too sick to go to the drugstore, too sick to walk, too sick to even move, the doctor may want you to come to his office right away and sit in the waiting room.

Assuming you can get to the doctor's office without dying, your first job is to find a good seat, ideally one that is close to the tropical-fish tank and as far as possible from patients with visible fungus. Then you should read an old copy of *National Geographic*. Doctors like to have *National Geographic* in their waiting rooms, because it reminds patients that in many primitive countries people are not fortunate enough to have the kind of medical care we have here in the U.S.A. Many patients feel so much better after reading it for a couple of hours that they don't even need to see the doctor. They just pay their bills and leave.

But if you still feel sick, the medical personnel will order you to undress and put on a garment that gives your secret bodily parts a high degree of visibility. Then they'll take some blood out of your arm and make you go into a bathroom and urinate into a glass container. While you're in there, the medical personnel will hide, giggling, in a closet, so that when you emerge you have to parade around, bodily parts flashing in every direction, looking for somebody to give the container to. None of this has anything to do with curing you. Why on earth would they want your blood and urine? They'll just throw it away. The point of all this is to determine whether you are really, sincerely sick, sick enough to actually see the doctor.

If you pass this test, you get to go into a little room and sit on a table covered with cold waxed paper for about forty-five minutes—this is the final test—while the doctor watches you through a secret peephole. If he is satisfied that you qualify, he'll bustle into the room and prod you with various implements, muttering all the while. The doctor is not allowed to tell you directly what is wrong—again, this would be a breach of ethics—so you have to listen closely to his muttering, and interpret it. Here are the standard doctor mutters, translated to laymen's terms:

• *"Uh-huh"*: This means "Oh my God."

- *"Ummm"*: This means "Good Lord."
- *"Ah hah"*: This means "I vaguely remember seeing a case like this in medical school, but it hadn't advanced nearly this far."

After the doctor has finished prodding you, either he will send you to the hospital, which will give you a battery of extremely humiliating tests designed to weed out people who are not serious about being hospitalized, or he will call the drugstore and order you a small bottle of pills that costs $34.38. If he spent much time in the Boy Scouts, he may also decide to apply a tourniquet.

"Great Baby! Delicious!"

I HAVE BEEN a father for nearly six months now, so needless to say I know virtually everything there is to know about raising babies. The main thing is discipline. You have to ignore all those bleeding-heart psychological theories about being sensitive to your baby's many delicate emotional wants. These theories are based on the insane premise that babies *have* many delicate emotional wants. In fact, babies have only one want, and it is hardly delicate: they want to put everything in the entire world except food into their mouths. As far as babies are concerned, the sole function of the world is to provide objects for them to drool on. If you were to open up a baby—and I am not for a minute suggesting that you should—you would find that 85 to 90 percent of the space reserved for bodily organs is taken up by huge, highly active drool glands. Scientists at a major scientific university recently conducted a study in which they collected, in scientific jars, all the drool that a six-month-old baby produced in one twenty-four-hour period. They were stunned at the result. Many of them had to go home and lie down.

The greatest threat to your baby is educational toys, which you are required by federal law to buy several dozen of. Educational toys are advertised in baby magazines, which arrive by the thousands in the mail when you have a baby. In a typical ad, a baby is looking thoughtfully (for a baby) at two pieces of plastic. According to the ad, the pieces of plastic are helping the baby "acquire skills of problem-solving." In fact, the only problem the baby is solving is the problem of how to get both pieces in its mouth. These so-called educational toys are merely encouraging your baby to act stupid.

This is dangerous. If you let your baby continue to stick things in his or her mouth, he or she will have a hard time in later life. I mean, suppose your child goes to a major Wall Street law firm for a job interview, and ends up putting all the waiting-room magazines and ashtrays in his or her mouth. He or she would make a poor impression, and would end up having to be a bum or work for the government.

So obviously, your job as a parent is to straighten your baby out. You'll have to be tough. Here's how I handle my five-and-a-half-month-old son: When he's lying on a blanket, putting various federally required educational toys in his mouth, I say firmly: "Robert, if you keep putting those educational toys in your mouth, I am not going to give you an allowance this week." If he doesn't respond to *that*, I up the ante. I say: "Robert, besides not giving you any allowance, I am not going to read to you from the famous Greek epic poem the

Iliad, usually ascribed to Homer." So far, Robert has continued to put educational toys in his mouth, but I think he's getting worried.

Of course, once you get your baby away from "educational" toys, you'll have to occupy it with new, more meaningful activities. The best activities are games. Here are some excellent, meaningful baby games designed by a distinguished panel of baby experts:

OKLAHOMA BABY CHICKEN HAT
Grasp your baby firmly and put it on your head like a hat, stomach down. Then stride around the room and cluck like a chicken to the tune of "Surrey with the Fringe on Top," bouncing in time to the music.

WILD TEENAGE BABIES FROM OUTER SPACE
Lie on your back and hold your baby over you, facing down; move it slowly up and down, like a flying saucer, making flying-saucer noises and feigning great fear when it appears to be about to land on the planet Earth.

(NOTE: Wear protective clothing for the preceding two games.)

ATTACK OF THE BABY EATERS
Lay the baby on the floor, face up. Announce that you are *very* hungry, and start nibbling at the baby's toes, then its hands, and finally, with great gusto, its stomach. Every now and then, yell: "Great baby! Delicious!"

These games will teach your baby many meaningful lessons, the main one being that the world is full of deranged people.

The only other major problem you'll have with your

baby is feeding it solid foods. Many kinds of baby food are available, all of them disgusting. Basically, the baby-food industry takes things that no normal human being would ever dream of eating, such as squash, and grinds them into mush and puts them in little jars. Babies, of course, hate baby food; they would much prefer the kinds of things *you* eat, such as cheeseburgers and beer. If we fed babies normal food, they would be full-grown, productive adults in a matter of weeks. But this would destroy the baby-food industry.

As I noted earlier, babies do not take solid food through their mouths, which are generally occupied with other objects. Babies absorb solid food through their chins. You can save yourself a lot of frustrating effort if you smear the food directly on your baby's chin, rather than putting it in the baby's mouth and forcing the baby to expel it on to its chin, as so many uninformed parents do.

Booosts and Baby Care

WARNING: This article contains the word breast. *I checked with an editor, and he said I could say "breast" as long as I used it scientifically, rather than to arouse prurient interest." For example, I could say: "Two breasts plus two breasts equals four breasts"; but I could not say: "Hey, get a load of that breast."*

Anyway, I just thought I'd warn you in case you don't want to read the word breast. *The rest of the article is about raising babies, and it's very informative, so for the benefit of those of you who want to read everything but the paragraph with "breast" in it, I'll let you know when you're about to come to it.*

THE MOST IMPORTANT THING to remember about raising your baby is that you must not take anyone's advice, except, of course, mine. Many people, such as your parents, will try to advise you, but you must ignore them. If they knew so much about raising kids, they wouldn't have screwed you up so badly.

Most people make babies out to be very complicated, but the truth is they have only three moods:

Mood One: Just about to cry.

Mood Two: Crying.

Mood Three: Just finished crying.

Your job, as a parent, is to keep the baby in Mood Three as much as possible; this means you have to figure out why it's crying. Here's a tip: Babies *never* cry because their diapers are dirty. You change their diapers only to make *yourself* feel better. You could leave the same diaper on your baby for *months* and it would be perfectly happy, although considerably heavier and less pleasant to be around.

So that leaves only two reasons your baby cries:

• It is hungry.

• Some other reason.

If your baby is hungry, you should feed it.

WARNING: The next paragraph is the one with "breast" in it. So you should either skip it or be prepared for some very explicit talk.

YOU CAN either bottle-feed or breast-feed your baby. Many noted health fanatics strongly recommend that you breast-feed your baby on the grounds that it is very good for the baby. This may be true, but the *real* advantage of breast-feeding is that *only female persons*

156

can do it. This means you male persons do not have to get up at the insane hours babies like to get up at. At first you may feel guilty about this, and you'll get up in the middle of the night to give the female person moral support. But after a while you'll get so good at morally supporting her that you'll be able to do it *without even waking up.* In the morning, when the female person is exhausted from lack of sleep, you can commiserate with her. You can say: "I know how you feel. This morally supporting is no bed of roses, either." She'll really appreciate hearing this.

If your baby doesn't stop crying after you feed it, it is crying for some other reason. You can try handing it back and forth and saying: "What do you suppose is wrong?" This does no good whatsoever, but it is an old traditional ritual and it passes the time. You can also try making funny faces; this teaches the baby that its parents may be brain-damaged. Or you can give the baby educational toys. My wife bought our baby several dozen expensive educational toys, designed by experts to teach babies about colors and spatial relationships and other vital educational things. Our baby ignores them. He could not be less interested in spatial relationships. The only toy he *really* likes is an extremely tacky plastic Wonder Bread wrapper, which he stares at happily for long periods. I'm growing fond of it myself.

Suet Won't Do It

MANY YEARS AGO, practically nobody in America had a weight problem, because almost everybody was an Indian, and all there was to eat was bison. The Indians had bison for breakfast, bison for lunch, and bison for supper. After a few thousand years of this, they mostly just picked at their food.

Then along came the early white settlers. They didn't have a weight problem either, because they were engaged in Westward Expansion, which consumes a great many calories. Also, the pioneers rarely got a chance to eat. Oh, they tried: they'd be crossing the Great Plains, and the wagonmaster would yell; "Okay, everyone, let's form the wagons into a circle for a snack." But before they could even get out the plates, the Indians, desperate for nonbison food, would attack. If the pioneers had been more thoughtful, they could have carried extra snacks, but they brought only enough for themselves, so unfortunately they had to kill the vast majority of the Indians.

Next the pioneers built farms, and soon the country was covered with amber fields of grain. As a result, everybody almost starved to death, because what the hell are you going to do with grain? Eat it? You'd be better off with bison. Fortunately, the farmers were able to sell their grain to the Russians, who will eat anything. In exchange, the Russians gave the farmers money, which the farmers used to buy food. So now we have tons of food, only nobody does any actual work except the farmers. Everybody else sits around offices and eats, which is why today most Americans are overweight, some of them to the point where they tend to stall escalators.

To figure out whether you are overweight, determine your sex and locate your correct scientific weight on this table:

SEX	CORRECT WEIGHT
Male	155 pounds
Female	115 pounds
Child	60 pounds

If you weigh more than you should, you can attempt to disguise it, but this rarely works. For example, I once worked in an office with an overweight woman. I can't remember her name, but it was an overweight name, like Bertha, so I'll call her that. Most of Bertha's overweight was concentrated in her behind. She looked like a perfectly normal person who for some reason was carrying an ottoman under her dress. Bertha had read in some beauty magazine that if you have a big behind, you should stand in such a way that one arm dangles in front of it, blocking the view. So Bertha made it a point to always have one arm dangling down, even when she was carrying heavy financial ledgers. She looked like she had some kind of nerve disorder. People were always saying "what's wrong with your arm, Bertha?" until finally it became blatantly obvious that she was trying to obscure her behind, which her arm was too small to do anyway unless she put on a catcher's mitt.

Another popular way to disguise excess weight is to wear clothing with vertical stripes. The idea is that vertical stripes create an optical illusion that makes you look thinner, but the truth is that they create an optical illusion that makes you look as though you were wearing a cafe awning. Also, every schoolchild knows that the only reason people wear vertical stripes is to disguise excess weight. You might just as well wear a big sign that says "FAT." What I'm driving at is that you can't really hide your weight problem, which

159

means that sooner or later you have to go on a diet.

IMPORTANT HEALTH NOTE:
Before you go on any diet, you should consult your
doctor, or at least send him some money.

The principle behind diets is that you cut down on the amount of calories you eat. A "calorie" is a unit of measurement that tells you how good food tastes. Really good food, like steak or fudge, has a very high calorie content; really awful food, like grapefruit halves, has almost no calories. (Now before I get a lot of outraged letters from citrus growers, let me point out that I am not opposed to grapefruit halves, except as food. I think grapefruit halves can serve many useful purposes around the home, such as extinguishing small fires.)

To understand how diets work, you have to understand how your body digests food. The process starts in your mouth, which tastes the food and covers it with spit, then sends it down to your stomach to be broken down for use as bodily parts. This is done by color. Red foods, such as rare steak, beets and Hawaiian Punch, are used to form red body parts, such as the heart; green foods, such as beans and lime Jell-O, are used to form green body parts, such as the kidney; beer is used to form urine; and so on. The problem is that if, on a given day, your body doesn't need any further parts, it turns the food into fat. Your body fully intends to go back to the fat someday and turn it into something useful, but it never gets a chance because you're always sliding more spit-covered food down your throat. So your fat just sits there, useless, until gradually it loses self-esteem and, desperate for

160

attention, starts interfering with the other organs. This is why you have to go on a diet.

Another principle behind diets is that you eat things that are so disgusting that your stomach rejects them and goes looking for fat to use as body parts. This is the big problem with diets! You spend a lot of time eating things like Melba toast. Melba toast was developed by the British, and it is not really food at all. You could airlift a thousand tons of Melba toast to some wretched, starving Asian village, and the starving Asians would use it to build homes or as bookmarks, but it would never occur to them to eat it. This is why diets don't work. You spend a couple of days eating Melba toast, then you lunge for the Twinkles, and you end up fatter than ever.

The only other way to lose weight is to go on a scientific weight-loss program. These are widely advertised in those newspapers they sell at supermarket checkout lines, the ones with headlines like: BURT REYNOLDS FINDS CANCER CURE IN UFO RIDE WITH PRINCESS DIANA.

You should buy one of these magazines and flip through the pages until you see a full-page advertisement with a headline that says WOMAN LOSES 240 POUNDS IN 30 SECONDS. Under the headline are two pictures of a woman's head: in the first picture the head is on top of what appears to be an industrial boiler wearing a 1952 bathing suit; in the second picture, the head is on top of Bo Derek. Under the picture it says: "Mrs. Earl Clamp of Wastewater, Tex., reports that the Amazing New Brand New Amazing Scientific 30-Second Weight-Loss Program saved her marriage and prevented serious damage to her home. Let Mrs. Clamp tell you about it in her own

161

words: 'Well, in my own words, I realized I had a serious weight problem one day when my husband, Earl, wanted to take me to the Recreational Vehicle and Rare Gem Show at the mall, and I couldn't get out the front door, so I decided to go out through the cellar doors, only I knocked over the water heater and the pipes broke and we had water all over Earl's pelt collection. So I said: "Earl, I'm going to try the Amazing New Brand New Amazing Scientific 30-Second Weight-Loss Program." I didn't think I could do it, but this program is so scientific that I lost 240 pounds in 30 seconds, right there in the basement. Now Earl is proud to show nude pictures of me to his friends.' "

I'M SURE these weight-loss programs work, because they have pictorial proof, and, besides, the supermarket checkout newspapers have a reputation for thoroughly checking everything for accuracy before they print it. Which is a lot more than you can say for this publication.

Dentistry Self•Drilled

I BET YOU rarely stop to think how important your teeth are. This is good. America is in enough trouble as it is, what with inflation and all; we just can't afford to have people stopping to think how important their teeth are, especially on major highways.

Nevertheless, you owe a lot to your teeth. They are your best friends. Think about it: while you're out here, playing tennis and reading novels, they're sitting patiently in your mouth, a foul-smelling, disgusting place almost devoid of recreational facilities, dealing with Slim Jims and Cheez-Its and the other crap you give them to chew.

You ought to apologize to your teeth for the way you treat them. You ought to go up to a mirror, right now, and bare your teeth and look them straight in their eyes and say: "I'm sorry." You may want to practice a bit so you can say this clearly with your teeth bared. Don't let the children see you.

Now I know what you're thinking. You're thinking: "I don't have to apologize to my teeth. I take good care of my teeth."

That's what *you* think. That's what *I* thought, too, until I started going to the dentist again recently after a brief absence of about twelve years. I stopped going because I didn't trust him. For one thing, he wore an outfit that buttoned on the side, the kind the spaceship crews wear in low-budget science fiction movies. For another thing, he and his cohorts *always left the room* when they X-rayed me. They'd make up flimsy excuses, like "I have to go put my socks in the dryer," or "I think the cat is throwing up." Then they'd flip the X-ray switch and race out of the room, probably to a lead-lined concrete bunker.

When he came back, the dentist would jab me in the gums sixty or seventy times until my mouth was full of blood and I had to spit in what appeared to be a miniature toilet. Then he'd show me what he claimed was an X-ray of my mouth, knowing full well I would not be able to distinguish an X-ray of my mouth from a color slide of the Parthenon, and he'd tell me I had a cavity and he was going to fill it. I would tell him I hadn't noticed any so-called cavity, and that it was, after all, *my* mouth. And he would give me this long routine about how if he didn't fill it, all my teeth would fall out and I'd lose my job and end up drooling on myself in a gutter, which is what they taught him to say in dental school. Then he would spend several hours drilling a hole in my tooth.

Answer me this: A cavity is a hole in your teeth, right? So if the dentist is so *upset* about this hole in your teeth, why does he spend so much time making it *bigger?* Huh? Does he need more money so he can buy more space-uniform shirts?

Finally I decided I could save some money if I stopped going to the dentist, got a sharp implement and, in the privacy of my own home, jabbed *myself* in the gums a couple of times a year. I figured I could ward off cavities by brushing after every meal with an effective decay-preventive dentifrice. I mean, that's what they told us for years, right? "Brush your teeth after every meal," they said. Parents said it. Teachers said it. Bucky Beaver said it.

Never trust a talking beaver. I found this out the hard way when, after twelve years of brushing like a madman, I returned to the dentist. The Dental Hygienist looked at my mouth the way you would look at a full spittoon. "You haven't been flossing," she said.

It seems that while I was home jabbing myself in the gums, the Dental Community was losing its enthusiasm for brushing and getting into flossing. These days the Dental Community regards anybody who merely brushes as a real bozo. This is blatantly unfair. In all those years of going to school and watching Bucky Beaver and Mister Tooth Decay, I never heard *one word* about flossing.

Flossing does not come naturally to human beings. If

the Good Lord had wanted us to floss our teeth, He would have given us less self-respect. But the Dental Community says we have to do it, because otherwise we'll get gum disease.

Pretty slick, isn't it? If we can't even see cavities, how the hell are we going to dispute them when they tell us we have gum disease?

I was about to point all this out to my dentist when he gave me this gas, nitrous oxide I believe, and all of a sudden I felt *great*. I began to really *appreciate* the Dental Community for coming up with flossing and all the other fine things it has done for me over the years. I even began to soften toward Bucky Beaver.

I think this was part of the plan.

Culture Staggers On

Art Cuts Really Sphinx

IF YOU ARE a member of the private sector, you are going to have to start supporting the arts.

For the benefit of those of you who do not know what sector you belong to, here is a simple way to figure it out: If you get Presidents' Day, election day, Arbor Day, Columbus Day, your birthday, Groundhog Day, and Flag Day off, you belong to the government sector. Otherwise, you belong to the private sector, and, as I said, you will have to start supporting the arts, because the government sector is cutting back.

The government sector took over the arts a few years back because the private sector had dropped the ball. The problem was that the private sector consisted largely of common people who spent most of their time working and, as a result, never became cultured. Their concept of "art" involved flamingo-shaped lawn ornaments, or pictures of dogs with actual working clocks in their stomachs. The only time that common people ever watched ballet was when it was on "The Ed Sullivan Show," and even then they watched it only because they knew it would last no more than three minutes and would be followed shortly by an act featuring monkeys wearing dresses.

This widespread lack of culture created a major problem for the few people who were interested in poetry, classical music, opera, ballet, sculpture, painting—in short, the real, serious, cultural, art-type activities that most people find fairly boring. The problem was that the common people would not voluntarily pay for these activities, so the only places where culture was available were:

- Junior high schools, where, under state law, children are required to do cultural things, such as screech away on rented violins, and parents are required to watch them, and
- New York City, where there are so many people that you can get a paying crowd for virtually anything, including opera and live nude dog wrestling.

But other than that, art was pretty scarce. Then some cultured person came up with a brilliant plan: If common people wouldn't support art voluntarily, why not *force* them to support it? Now when I say "force," I'm not talking about just walking up to some common person and ordering him, at gunpoint, to attend an opera. What I'm talking about is getting the government to *tax* common people, then use their money to put on an opera.

Actually, this is an old, tried-and-true way to support the arts, dating back to the ancient Egyptians. How do you think the Egyptians built the Sphinx? Surely, you don't think that a bunch of common Egyptians just got together one day and said: "Hey, why don't we build a Sphinx?" Of course not. Left to their own devices, the common Egyptians would have spent their time growing food. To get some real *culture,* to get the *Sphinx,* the Egyptians needed a government authority, someone with vision, someone with taste, someone with whips and spears.

Our government's approach to the arts is essentially the same, but less messy. Unlike the ancient Egyptians, we common people are not forced to attend cultural activities: we are merely forced to pay for them. This works out much better. You see, under the Egyptian method, you always had a bunch of sweating or dead Egyptians around your Sphinx; under our method, cultured people can have an opera in the Kennedy Center in Washington, safe in the knowledge that few, if any, of the common people who paid for it will show up to watch. After all, a lot of the common people live thousands of miles away; they couldn't attend even if they wanted to.

For a while there, our government was in the art business whole hog, forking over hundreds of millions of dollars for art. But now the program is in trouble. Jimmy Carter wanted to spend about $300 million on art this year, but Ronald Reagan thinks it should spend only about half that, so he'll have more money to spend on exploding objects. Needless to say, the art officials are extremely upset. Their position is extremely logical: they argue that if the government is going to spend hundreds of billions of dollars on things designed to kill people, it should spend at *least* $300 million for art that people don't want to see.

But it looks as though the art officials are going to lose, and that means that, unless somebody does something, art will fall back into the hands of the lawn-flamingo owners. So it's up to us public-spirited, private-sector people to pick up the ball. We've got to develop some way to make sure people attend operas and ballets, look at paintings, read poetry, and so on. Maybe we should set up a system patterned after volunteer fire departments: whenever anybody discovered a cultural activity, he could sound an alarm, and the public-spirited citizens in the area would go and watch it. If we all work together, we might be able to keep art alive, even without the government. Maybe we could even build a sphinx.

Some Art, Some Art Not

I AM EXTREMELY fond of art. Whenever I have a few spare moments, there's nothing I enjoy more than hauling out a batch of art and looking at it. This is probably because I was exposed to so much art when I was in grade school. At least once a year, the teachers would herd us kids into a bus and take us to a museum and expose us to thousands of square yards of old paintings. We were very impressed, particularly because many of these paintings featured enormous naked women, women with thighs the size of fully inflated life rafts, lounging around and eating fruit.

The reason that this theme is so common in old paintings is that years ago Europe was terrorized by packs of enormous naked women. They would stride into a town, munching on pears, and threaten to knock down the cathedral if their portraits weren't painted immediately. Eventually they were driven off by a particularly harsh winter, but their paintings are still popular today because they offer such a good value in terms of square yards of painting per dollar.

Which brings us to money. Money is very important to the art world, because without it we would have no way to know how good a particular piece of art is. For example, let's say that we want to decide which painting is better: the *Mona Lisa* by Leonardo da Vinci, or *Aristotle Contemplating the Bust of Homer* by Rembrandt (whose first name was Beauregard, which is why he never used it). Now let's say that the list price on the *Mona Lisa* is $36 million, whereas the price on *Aristotle* etc. is $12 million. This would tell your experienced art critic that the *Mona Lisa* is three

172

times as good, artwise, as *Aristotle* etc. and nearly six million times as good as those paintings they sell in shopping malls, the ones that feature children with enormous brown eyes who are supposed to look helpless and appealing but actually look like some sort of bizarre species of insect.

THE HISTORY OF ART

The first art was created by primitive people, who made pots and plates with primitive decorations. They didn't realize this was art. They thought it was just pots and plates. Their problem was that seconds after they made a pot or plate, an archaeologist would race up and snatch it and put it in a museum. The primitive people tried all kinds of schemes to protect their pots and plates, including burying them, but the archaeologists would just dig them up. Finally, with nothing to cook in or eat from, the primitive people starved to death and became extinct.

The next big trend in art was painting, which was invented because wealthy people needed something to put on their walls. One famous painter, Michelangelo (first name, Buford), even painted on the ceiling. This was before the discovery of acoustical tiles. In those days, everybody painted the same subject, which was Mother and Child. That was a really popular item. Occasionally, an artist would try something different, such as Mother and Trowel, or Mother and Labrador Retriever, but they never sold.

After the Mother and Child Phase came the Enormous Naked Women Eating Fruit Phase, which was followed by the Just Plain Fruit with No Women of Any Kind Phase and the Famous Kings and Dukes Wearing Silly Outfits Phase. All of these phases were part of the Sharp and Clear School of painting, which means that even though the subjects were boring, they were at least recognizable. The Sharp and Clear School ended with Vincent Van Gogh, who invented the Fuzzy but Still Recognizable School and cut off his ear. This led to the No Longer Recognizable at All School, and finally the Sharp and Clear Again but Mostly Just Rectangles School, which is the school that is popular today, except at shopping malls.

HOW TO APPRECIATE ART

The number one rule of art appreciation is that you never ever bring up the issue of whether or not a particular piece of art is attractive. Let's say you're looking at a painting of two large green rectangles. If you say something like, "Those two large green rectangles are very attractive," people will realize immediately that you do not appreciate art. What you want to say is: "Using the tension created by the contrast in line, shape and tone, offset by the almost deliberately simplistic linearity of hue, the artist subtly, yet inevitably, leads the viewer to a greater awareness of the need for more controls over the acquisition and use of our nation's mineral resources, particularly zinc." This particular sentence will work on almost any brand of art except enormous naked women, who obviously have nothing to do with zinc.

Music to Get Rich By

BASICALLY, THERE are two kinds of music:

• "Classical" music, which is the kind written by dead German guys and played by people wearing tuxedos.

• "Regular" music, which can be written by anybody and played by anybody and gets on the radio a lot.

If you want to make large sums of money, you should get into regular music. These days classical music is popular with only about three hundred people, the same ones who contribute voluntarily to public television. Classical music tends to go on for days, which is why it is played by "orchestras," or groups of four hundred fifty to five hundred people whose parents made them practice classical music when all the other kids were out learning how to French-kiss. Orchestra people divide up the labor: one group will play a batch of music, or "movement," then everybody sits back and reads magazines from little magazine stands while the "conductor" consults his notes and decides which musicians will play next. Sometimes the conductor singles out a musician who has been chewing gum or fooling around and forces him or her to play all alone while the other musicians snicker. If you ever have to be in an orchestra, you should try to sit in back, near the guy who plays the triangle. You'll hardly ever get called on.

Music scholars divide orchestra instruments into five families:

• Instruments You Blow into and Eventually Have to Get the Spit out of (tubas, whistles, cormorants, tribunes).

• Instruments You Hit (drums, triangles, rhomboids, homophones).

• Instruments That Are Easily Concealed (piccolos).

• Furniture (pianos).

• Instruments That Could Turn out to Be Worth a Million Skillion Dollars (violins). The really valuable violins are the ones made by Antonius Stradivarius, which are prized because they were made with exquisite care and craftsmanship and each one contains just over seventeen ounces of pure heroin in a secret compartment which you open by pressing with your chin.

Classical music gradually lost popularity because it is too complicated: you need twenty-five or thirty skilled musicians just to hum it properly. So people began to develop regular music. The most profitable kind of regular music is rock 'n' roll.

Rock 'n' roll comes from the blues, a kind of music developed by American slaves. It is called the "blues" because it is very sad. Evidently the slaves found slavery depressing. Blues lyrics generally go like this:

> *My woman she done left me*
> *My children left me too*
> *My mule done kicked my kidneys*
> *And my income tax is due*

For a long time, blues music was popular only with black people, who were then known as "Negroes." Black blues musicians played in lowdown bars for very little money. Then, in the early 1950s, young white people got interested in the blues. They developed a modified version called "rock 'n' roll," which became enormously popular and turned many of them into millionaires. They routinely paid homage to the black blues musicians who paved the way for them, who made it all possible, and who continued to play in lowdown bars for very little money.

The principal difference between rock 'n' roll and classical music is that your average piece of classical music has about a dozen melodies and no words, whereas your average rock 'n' roll song has one melody (sometimes less) and about a dozen words. When rock 'n' roll composers are in a hurry to finish songs so they can get to important luncheon dates, they sometimes make up some of the words. Take, for example, the words to the 1960s hit rock ''n' roll song "Sittin' in La La":

> *Sittin' in la la waitin' for my ya ya*
> *Uh huh, uh huh*
> *Sittin' in la la waitin' for my ya ya*
> *Uh huh, uh huh*

Probably the composer planned to go back and put in real words for "la la" and "ya ya," but before he could get around to it somebody released the song and it sold several million records. Another example is "Land of a Thousand Dances," whose composer evidently got called away to an urgent appointment after he had written only two words:

> *I said na na na na na*
> *Na na na na na na na na na na*
> *Na na na na*

THE OTHER KINDS of regular music you can make money from are country music, which is popular with people who like songs about drunken infidelity but requires singers with funny clothes and Southern accents; big-band music, which is popular with people

177

who like big bands but requires big bands; and easy-listening music, which is popular in elevators and supermarkets but can be sung only by groups of heavily sedated suburbanites. You should steer clear of jazz, opera, folk, marching-band and bagpipe music: the market for these is minuscule. You will never see hordes of fans clamoring for the autograph of a bagpiper.

HOW TO READ MUSIC

Anyone can read music. It's simply a matter of memorizing the various notes and musical signs. The major notes are:

dum

da

de

tra

tra-la

The major musical signs are:

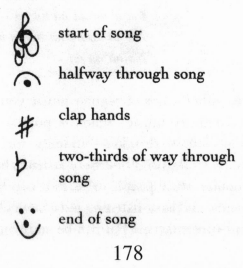

start of song

halfway through song

clap hands

two-thirds of way through song

end of song

Okay, now let's try reading a real piece of music:

CORRECT ANSWER: "TRA-LA DUM DE DUM DUM (CLAP) DA DUM"

Prurient Interest Rate

FIRST, LET ME make it clear that I am opposed to pornography. I believe if God wanted people to be seen naked, He would not have made so many of them unattractive. Nevertheless, I feel compelled to write about pornography, because it is directly related to the increase in drug abuse, unemployment, international terrorism, all-polyester clothing, and, above all, violence. This was a far less violent country in the days when pornography was illegal, unless you count the Civil War. Pornography is like tooth decay, eating slowly away at the molars of our morals, and if it is not stopped, we will wind up as a toothless nation, gumming at the raw meat of international competition while the drool of decadence dribbles down our collective chin and messes up the clean tablecloth of our children's futures.

The dictionary tells us that the word *pornography* comes from the Greek words *porno,* meaning

179

"publications," and *graphy,* meaning "that adolescent males gather around in junior high school halls and snicker at." The problem is that this simple definition is inadequate for the legal authorities, who need something less comprehensible. So for the past twenty years or so, the legal authorities have spent enormous amounts of time and effort gathering up and scrutinizing dirty books, trying to come up with a suitable definition of pornography so they can throw people in jail for selling it. The dirty books are scrutinized first by the police, then by the district attorney, then by a local judge and jury, then by some appeals judges, and then finally, when the really pornographic pages are dog-eared from all this intense legal scrutiny, the books are shipped in unmarked crates to the U.S. Supreme Court, where the justices sit around in their robes and discuss them:

CHIEF JUSTICE: Okay, we have here the case of *Nebraska v. The Huge Boar Adult Book Store and Health Spa,* which is accused of selling an illustrated publication entitled *Young Teenaged Baby-Sitters with Flawless Skin Go to Daytona Beach* to eight undercover agents on July 3, 1972. Have you all scrutinized the evidence?

OTHER JUSTICES *(crowding around the evidence)*: Not yet! Not yet! We're still scrutinizing, and—My God! Look at this photograph! It looks like a—No, it can't be—Yes, it is! It's a—

CHIEF JUSTICE: Now as I interpret the First Amendment, the issue here is—

OTHER JUSTICES: —it's a *Flamingo!* Incredible! I mean, I know flamingos thrive in captivity, but I had no *idea.* That—

180

CHIEF JUSTICE: Whether the constitutional guarantee of free speech conflicts with the—

OTHER JUSTICES: How do you suppose they got all that Cool Whip to adhere to the ceiling?

After a few sessions like this, the justices render a decision, which says: "Having reviewed the evidence in this case, the court finds that, inasmuch as the prothonotary nature of the alleged violation precludes a pro forma elucidation of its meretriciousness or meritoriousness per se, it cannot be determined whether such alleged violation may or may not be deleterious without a heck of a lot more scrutiny by the members of the court."

Since nobody ever has the vaguest idea what the justices mean, their decisions always set off a new round of arrests and scrutiny throughout the legal system, which by now has accumulated over thirty million cubic yards of evidence suspected of being pornographic. Eventually, the national stockpile will get so large that the authorities will have to start giving pornography away to poor people, the way they did with cheese.

Years ago, the pornography industry was fairly small, because people were ashamed to be caught reading dirty books and magazines. Then along came Hugh Hefner, who had a dream: to publish a cultured, sophisticated magazine, a magazine with in-depth interviews of influential people, with top-notch fiction, with thought-provoking articles, with pictures of large-breasted women either naked or dressed up as bunny rabbits. The beauty of Hugh's idea was that you could pretend you were buying his magazine to read the thought-provoking articles. You could grab an issue of

Playboy and say "I'm very eager to read this interview with Albert Schweitzer," knowing full well that it is very difficult to read any magazine when you hold it sideways, which is how people generally hold *Playboy*.

Hugh's mistake is that he started to believe that *Playboy* really *was* a cultured, sophisticated magazine, and he started writing these enormous, droning articles about his philosophy of life. This was a stupid mistake. I mean, it's not as if thousands of *Playboy* readers wrote in and said: "Hey, Hugh, enough with all these big-breasted naked women. What's your philosophy of life?" But he published his philosophy anyway, and it took up many pages of valuable space that could have been used for naked women. Soon competitors sprung up, and now you can't walk into a convenience store without seeing dozens of magazines like *Hustler, Rogue, Gallery, Nugget,* and *Newsweek. Newsweek* got into the market just recently, when it published a picture of a seminaked woman on the cover. It's a small start, but if it works out, I suspect that in a couple of years *Newsweek* will start telling us its philosophy of life, and people will be holding it sideways. If it plays its cards right, it might even get scrutinized by the Supreme Court.

Compressed Classics

ONE EFFECTIVE technique for avoiding boring conversations on airplanes is to pull an extremely sharp ax out of your briefcase and spend the entire flight fondling it and muttering. Of course, to get the ax onto the airplane, you'll have to convince the airport security people that you're not a hijacker:

SECURITY PERSON: Excuse me, sir, but there's an extremely sharp ax in your briefcase.

YOU: Yes, I need it for my business. I'm an ax murderer.

SECURITY PERSON: Oh, okay. Sorry to inconvenience you, but we have to be on the lookout for hijackers. It's for your own protection.

YOU: Of course. Keep up the good work.

The only problem with the ax approach is that it tends to make the flight attendants skittery, and you may be forced to waste valuable time dealing with large numbers of armed law enforcement personnel after you land. So the technique I use to ward off boring conversations is to carry a book, which I pull out the instant a boring person tries to talk to me:

BORING PERSON: Hi. Where are you headed?

ME: Detroit.

BORING PERSON: No kidding? That's where *I'm* headed.

ME: What an astounding coincidence. And here we are, sitting together on a plane bound for Detroit, the very place we're both headed. I think I'll read my book now.

THE PROBLEM HERE is that you have to actually read the book, which may turn out to be even more boring than the person you're sitting next to, because, as a rule, books contain far too many words. For example, I was recently on a flight to St. Louis, unaware that my suitcase was going to get off at Indianapolis (apparently on the theory that all Midwestern cities are basically the same), and I read a new book about James Bond, the famous spy. I thought there would be no new James Bond books, because the person who wrote them is dead, but evidently the folks in the publishing world decided that if the original author was inconsiderate enough to die, then by God they would find somebody else to write his books for him. I think they're on to something. I think they ought to use the same approach with other famous dead authors, such as William Shakespeare:

The Warble, Peddle, and Leek Publishing Company proudly announces Romeo and Juliet II—*a sweeping saga of lust and passion that begins where the best-selling original left off. The story begins with the discovery that the two lovers didn't really stab themselves hard enough to die, and follows them through their lustful and passionate efforts to escape the clutches of their warring families and find a peaceful life of lust and passion! Now on sale at every drugstore and supermarket in the world.*

"*. . . better than the original!*"—Bullock, Missouri, Herald Gazette Chronicle Bugle.

"*. . . lustful . . . passionate!*"—Field and Stream.

"*. . . a recently published book!*"—The New York Times.

WELL ANYWAY, I was reading this James Bond book, and right away I realized that, like most books, it had too many words. The plot was the same one that all James Bond books have: An evil person tries to blow up the world, but James Bond kills him and his henchmen and makes love to several attractive women. There, that's it: twenty-four words. But the guy who wrote the book took *thousands* of words to say it. I mean, he never just writes: "Bond walked into the bedroom." Instead, he writes: "Bond eased the bedroom door latch open gently, praying that the click of the Zuch-Sweiss

184

stainless-steel door latch would not disturb the other inhabitants, and cautiously eyed the room, which he noted was paneled with European birch, or *Betula verrucosa*, probably from the Vorarlburg region of western Austria." And it goes on like this for *pages* before Bond gets around to killing a henchman. I could barely wade through it. I was tempted to start chatting with the person next to me about how we were both going to St. Louis.

And it's not just spy novels. Most books are too long. I remember in college when I had to read *The Brothers Karamazov* by the famous Russian alcoholic Fyodor Dostoyevsky. It's about these two brothers who kill their father. Or maybe only one of them kills the father. It's almost impossible to tell, because what they mostly do is talk for nearly a thousand pages. If all Russians talked as much as the brothers Karamazov did, I don't see how they found time to become a major world power.

Our literature professor told us that Dostoyevsky wrote *The Brothers Karamazov* to raise the question of whether there is a God. So what I want to know is, why didn't Dostoyevsky just come right out and *ask?* Why didn't he write:

> *Dear Reader:*
>   *Is there a God? It sure beats the heck out of me.*
>
>   *Sincerely,*
>   *Fyodor Dostoyevsky*

Here are some other famous works of literature that could easily have been summarized in a few words:

- *Moby-Dick*—Don't mess around with large whales, because they symbolize nature and will kill you.

- *A Tale of Two Cities*—French people are crazy.

- *Every poem ever written*—Poets are extremely sensitive.

Think of all the valuable time we would save if authors got right to the point this way. People would be able to read several dozen great books in a matter of minutes. College would take about two weeks. We'd all have more time for more important activities, such as reading newspaper columns.

A Little Learning ° ° °

Basic Frog Glop

A DISTINGUISHED, HIGH-LEVEL, blue-ribbon federal panel of people wearing suits recently released a report concluding that (and here I quote directly): "The American public education system has done just about as good a job of educating the nation's children as might be expected from a bucket of live bait." The report presented some shocking statistics to support this finding:

• For the past eleven years, American students have scored lower on standardized tests than European students, Japanese students, and certain species of elk;
• Seventy-eight percent of America's school principals have, at some point in their careers, worn white belts or shoes to school;
• Nobody in the entire United States remembers the exact date of the signing of the Treaty of Ghent.

The bottom line is that the educational system, which costs over $200 billion a year, is an unmitigated disaster. This is good news for everybody. It's good news for those of us who went to high school back when the schools were supposed to be better, because we can feel superior to today's students. When we go to shopping malls and see batches of teenagers standing around and laughing in a carefree teenaged manner, we can reassure ourselves by saying: "Those kids may be attractive and slim and healthy, and they may have their entire lives ahead of them and no gum problems whatsoever, but by God they never learned how to conjugate the verb 'to squat' in Latin, the way I had to when I was in school."

The panel's report is also good news for the kids, because it confirms their suspicion that they wouldn't have learned anything even if they had been paying attention in class instead of trying to see who could most accurately guess how large, in square inches, the sweat stain under the teacher's left armpit would be by the time the bell rang.

But most of all, the panel's report is good news for the teachers, school administrators, and other members of the American educational establishment, because as the people most responsible for screwing up the educational system in the first place, they will naturally expect to be given a great deal more money to fix it.

So everybody is pleased as punch to have blue-ribbon federal proof that the school system stinks on ice, and everybody is busy coming up with helpful suggestions for making the schools good again, the way they were when they were turning out real geniuses like the people who are making the suggestions. For example, President Reagan checked in from the planet Saturn with the suggestion that we need to go back to voluntary prayer in the schools. Now I think we can all agree that making our children pray voluntarily will certainly help, but we need to do more. We need to get Back to the Basics, back to the kinds of learning activities you and I engaged in.

For example, every student in the country should be required to read *Ethan Frome* unless he or she has a written doctor's excuse. As you no doubt vaguely recall, *Ethan Frome* is a book you had to read when you studied early American novels because it turns out there were hardly any good early American novels. As

190

I remember the plot, Ethan Frome falls in love with this woman, so they decide to crash into a tree on a sled. The sled crash is the only good part, and it lasts only about a page. But the way I look at it, if *I* had to read *Ethan Frome,* I don't see why these little snots today should get out of it.

They should also be forced to disassemble frogs, the way we did in biology. Remember? You'd slice your frog up with a razor and root around inside, looking for the heart and the kidney and the other frog organs that were clearly drawn in several colors in the biology textbook, until eventually you realized that you must have been issued a defective frog, because all you could ever find inside was frog glop. So you just poked at the glop for a while and then drew the heart, et cetera, from the biology textbook. This taught you about life. When I was in school, I also had to do a worm, although I'm not suggesting that all of today's students should have to do worms. Maybe just the really disruptive ones.

So that's my back-to-basics program: *Ethan Frome*, frogs, and maybe some class discussion of the cosine. And any kid who doesn't know the exact date of the signing of the Treaty of Ghent (December 24, 1814) will be held back for another year, or, if the Russians appear to be getting ahead of us in space again, shot.

Schools Not So Smart

ONE OF THE MORE popular ways to feel superior these days is to complain about the schools. We adults just *love* to drone on about how much better educated we are than our kids. We say stuff like: "These kids today.

They get out of high school and they don't even know how to read and write. Why, in my day we read *Moby-Dick* eighty-four times in the fourth grade alone." And so on. Adults just eat this kind of talk right up.

Well, I hate to disillusion everybody, but it's all a crock. We aren't better educated than our kids: they're just less drivel-oriented.

The main evidence adults offer to prove kids are less educated is the fact that Scholastic Aptitude Test (SAT) scores are declining. You remember SATs. You got your number-two pencils and sat in the cafeteria for two hours answering questions like this:

Fred wants to redo his bathroom in pink wallpaper, so he invites Sam over to help. If Fred's bathroom is eight feet by five feet and had a seven-foot ceiling, and each roll of wallpaper is thirty-two inches wide, how long will Sam take to realize there is something just a little bit strange about Fred?

SAT tests are designed by huge panels of experts in education and psychology who work for *years* to design tests in which *not one single question measures any bit of knowledge that anyone might actually need in the real world.* We should *applaud* kids for getting lower scores.

When you and I were in high school, we thought we had to learn all that crap so we could get into college and get good jobs and houses with driveways. The problem is that so many of us went to college that college degrees became as common, and as valuable, as bowling trophies. Kids today are smart enough not to waste brain cells trying to figure out how long Train A will take to overtake Train B just so they can go to college. That's why so many colleges are desperate for students. Any day now you'll be watching a late movie on television and you'll see this ad:

"Hi! I'm Huntingdon Buffington Wellington the Fourth, dean of admissions at Harvard University. I'll bet more than once you've said: 'I sure would like to go to a big-time Ivy League university, but I lack the brains, the background, and the requisite number of dinner jackets.' Well, this is your lucky day, because Harvard University is having its semiannual Standards Reduction Days. That's right: we're admitting people we once wouldn't have allowed to work in our boiler room. And for the first one hundred applicants who call our toll-free number, we're offering absolutely free this honorary degree written in *genuine Latin words.*"

ANOTHER REASON you shouldn't feel better educated than your kids is that almost everything your teachers told you is a lie. Take the continents. I bet they told you Europe was one continent, and Asia was another. Well, any moron with a map can plainly see *Europe and Asia are on the same continent.* I don't know who started the lunatic rumor that they were two continents. I suspect it was the French, because they wouldn't want to be on the same continent with, say, the Mongolians.

And what about those maps they showed you? Greenland looked *enormous,* bigger than Russia. If Greenland were *really* that big, it would be a Major Power. All the other nations would stay up late nights worrying about it. But the truth is Greenland is smallish and insignificant. The other nations rarely even invite it to parties.

So don't think your so smart.

Why We Don't Read

EVERY SO OFTEN I see a news article in which some educator gets all wrought up about the fact that people don't read books anymore:

WASHINGTON (Associated Press)—Noted educator Dr. Belinda A. Burgeon-Wainscot, speaking before the American Association of People Who Use the Title "Doctor" Even Though They Are Not Physicians, but Merely Graduate School Graduates, Which Are as Common These Days as Milkweed Pollen (AAPWUTDETTANPBMGSGWAACTDAMP), said today that people don't read books anymore. At least that's what we here at the Associated Press think she said. She spoke for about two hours, and used an awful lot of big words, and frankly we dozed off from time to time.

Well, I am not a noted educator, but I know why most of us don't read books. We don't read books because, from the very beginning of our school careers, noted educators have made us read books that are either boring or stupid and often both. Here's what I had to read in first grade:

"Look, Jane," said Dick. "Look Look Look. Look."
"Oh," said Jane. "Oh. Oh Oh Oh Oh Oh. Look."
"Oh," said Spot. "Oh my God."

Now I'm not claiming that we first-graders were a bunch of geniuses, but we didn't spend the bulk of the day saying "Look," either. We thought Dick and Jane were a drag, so many of us turned to comic books, which were much more interesting and informative.

When I was in first grade, the Korean War was going on, so I read comic books with names like "GI Combat Death Killers," featuring American soldiers with chin stubble who fought enemy Communist Orientals with skin the color of school buses. These comic books had lots of new and exciting words:

"Commie attack! Hit the dirt!"
BUDDA-BUDDA-BUDDA-BUDDA
"Grenade! Grenade!"
WHOOOOOOOOOOOOOOOMKABOOOOOOM
"Joe! They got Joe! Eat lead, you Reds!"
BUDDA-BUDDA-BUDDA-BUDDA-BUDDA
"Aieeeeeeeeeee."

And so on. This is how we developed our language skills? If we had stuck with Dick and Jane, we'd have sounded like morons.

After the first grade, our school books got longer, but they did not get more interesting. The history books were the worst. Take, for example, the Civil War. I think we can safely assume that the Civil War was fairly lively, but you would never know this from reading elementary school history books:

THE CIVIL WAR

The Civil War was very serious. It was caused by slavery and states' rights, and it resulted in the Gettysburg Address.

Discussion Questions: How serious was the Civil War? Would you feel nervous if you had to give the Gettysburg Address? Explain.

THE OTHER BIG PROBLEM with history textbooks was that they always started at the Dawn of Civilization and ended around 1948. So we'd spend the first three months of each school year reading about the ancient Sumerians at a leisurely pace. Then the teacher would realize that time was running short, and we'd race through the rest of history, covering World War II in a matter of minutes, and getting to Harry Truman on the last day. Then the next year, we'd go back to the ancient Sumerians. After a few years of this, we began to see history as an endlessly repeating, incredibly dull cycle, starting with Sumerians and leading inexorably to Harry Truman, then going back again. No wonder so many of us turned to loud music and drugs.

Things were a little better in English class, because we didn't have to read the same books over and over. On the other hand, we had to read a lot of books nobody would want to read even once, such as *The Last of the Mohicans,* which was written by James Fenimore Cooper, although I seriously doubt that Cooper himself ever read it. We also read a batch of plays by Shakespeare, which are very entertaining when you watch actors perform them but are almost impossible to understand when you read them:

FLAVORUS: Forsooth 'twixt consequence doest thou engage?

Wouldst thou thine bodkin under thee enrage?

HORACLES: In faith I wouldst not e'er intent fulfill, For o'er petards a dullard's loath to till.

(Shakespeare wrote this way because English was not his native language. He was Sumerian.)

Anyway, that's why I think people don't read books anymore. The sad thing is that there are many fine books around, just waiting to be read. You can see them on convenient display racks at any of the better supermarkets; they have titles like *The Goodyear Blimp Diet* and *Evil Nazi War Criminals Get an Atomic Bomb and Threaten to Destroy Uruguay.* These books are easy to read, and minutes after you read one you're ready for another. What we need is some kind of federal program to get people interested in them. Maybe the President could read some of them aloud on national television (he is very good at reading aloud). Or maybe we could give people an additional tax exemption for every book report they attach to their income tax returns. Whatever we do, we should do it soon, to get people out of the habit of getting all their information from television and poorly researched newspaper columns.

What Is and Ain't Grammatical

I CANNOT OVEREMPHASIZE the importance of good grammar.

What a crock. I could easily overemphasize the importance of good grammar. For example, I could say: "Bad grammar is the leading cause of slow, painful death in North America" or "Without good grammar, the United States would have lost World War Two."

The truth is that grammar is not the most important thing in the world. The Super Bowl is the most important thing in the world. But grammar is still important. For example, suppose you are being interviewed for a job as an airplane pilot, and your prospective employer asks you if you have any experience, and you answer: "Well, I ain't never actually flied no actual airplanes or nothing, but I got

197

several pilot-style hats and several friends who I like to talk about airplanes with."

If you answer this way, the prospective employer will immediately realize that you have ended your sentence with a preposition. (What you should have said, of course, is "several friends with who I like to talk about airplanes.") So you will not get the job, because airline pilots have to use good grammar when they get on the intercom and explain to the passengers that, because of high winds, the plane is going to take off several hours late and land in Pierre, South Dakota, instead of Los Angeles.

We did not always have grammar. In medieval England, people said whatever they wanted, without regard to rules, and as a result they sounded like morons. Take the poet Geoffrey Chaucer, who couldn't even spell his first name right. He wrote a large poem called *Canterbury Tales,* in which people from various professions—knight, monk, miller, reever, riveter, eeler, diver, stevedore, spinnaker, et cetera—drone on and on like this:

> *In a somer sesun whon softe was the sunne*
> *I kylled a younge birde ande I ate it on a bunne.*

When Chaucer's poem was published, everybody read it and said: "My God, we need some grammar around here." So they formed a Grammar Commission, which developed the parts of speech, the main ones being nouns, verbs, predicants, conjectures, particles, proverbs, adjoiners, coordinates, and rebuttals. Then the commission made up hundreds and hundreds of grammar rules, all of which were strictly enforced.

When the colonists came to America, they rebelled

against British grammar. They openly used words like "ain't" and "finalize," and when they wrote the Declaration of Independence they deliberately misspelled many words. Thanks to their courage, today we Americans have only two rules of grammar:

Rule 1. The word me is always incorrect.

Most of us learn this rule as children, from our mothers. We say things like: "Mom, can Bobby and me roll the camping trailer over Mrs. Johnson's cat?" And our mothers say: "Remember your grammar, dear. You mean: 'Can Bobby and *I* roll the camping trailer over Mrs. Johnson's cat?' Of course you can, but be home by dinnertime."

The only exception to this rule is in formal business writing, where instead of "I" you must use "the undersigned." For example, this business letter is incorrect:

"Dear Hunky-Dory Canned Fruit Company: A couple days ago my wife bought a can of your cling peaches and served them to my mother who has a weak heart and she damn near died when she bit into a live grub. If I ever find out where you live, I am gonna whomp you on the head with a ax handle."

This should be corrected as follows:

". . . If the undersigned ever finds out where you live, the undersigned is gonna whomp you on the head with a ax handle."

Rule 2. You're not allowed to split infinitives.

An infinitive is the word *to* and whatever comes right behind it, such as "to a tee," "to the best of my ability," "tomato," et cetera. Splitting an infinitive is putting something between the "to" and the other words. For example, this is incorrect:

"Hey man, you got any, you know, spare change you could give to, like, me?"

The correct version is:

". . . spare change you could, like, give to me?"

The advantage of American English is that, because there are so few rules, practically anybody can learn to speak it in just a few minutes. The disadvantage is that Americans generally sound like jerks, whereas the British sound really smart, especially to Americans. That's why Americans are so fond of those British dramas they're always showing on public television, the ones introduced by Alistair Cooke. Americans *love* people who talk like Alistair Cooke. He could introduce old episodes of "Hawaii Five-O" and Americans would think they were extremely enlightening.

So the trick is to use American grammar, which is simple, but talk with a British accent, which is impressive. This technique is taught at all your really snotty private schools, where the kids learn to sound like Elliot Richardson. Remember Elliot? He sounded extremely British, and as a result he got to be Attorney General, Secretary of State, Chief Justice of the Supreme Court, and Vice President *at the same time*.

You can do it, too. Practice in your home, then approach someone on the street and say: "Tally-ho, old chap. I would consider it a great honour if you would favour me with some spare change." You're bound to get quick results.

It Takes a Lot of Gaul

ONE OF THE MOST USELESS classes I ever took in high school, ranking right up there with calculus, was French. I took several years of French, and I learned hundreds of phrases, not one of which I would ever actually want to say to anybody. For example, my French teachers insisted that when I met a French person I should say *"Comment allez-vous?"* It turns out that this means "How do you go?" which is not the kind of thing you say when you want to strike someone as being intelligent. Your average French person already thinks most Americans are idiots, and you're not going to improve his opinion much if you barge up on him on some Paris street and start spewing high school French phrases:

YOU: *Comment allez-vous?* ("How do you go?")

FRENCH PERSON: *Je vais à pied, évidemtment. Vous devez avoir les cerveaux d'une truite.* ("I go on foot, obviously. You must have the brains of a trout.")

YOU: *Où est la bibliothèque?* ("Where is the library?")

FRENCH PERSON: *Partez, s'il vous plait. J'ai un fusil.* ("Please go away. I have a gun.")

MY WIFE DIDN'T DO ANY BETTER in high school French. She learned to say *"Je me suis cassé la jambe"* ("I have broken my leg") and *"Elle n'est pas jolie"* ("She is not pretty"). What on earth is she supposed to do with these phrases? I mean, suppose she does go to France and break her leg:

MY WIFE: *Je me suis cassé la jambe.* ("I have broken

201

my leg.")

FRENCH BYSTANDERS: *C'est dommage.* ("What a pity.")

MY WIFE: *Elle n'est pas jolie.* ("She is not pretty.")

FRENCH BYSTANDERS: *Bien, excusez-nous pour vivre. Vous n'êtes pas un grand prix vous-même.* ("Well, excuse us for living. You are no great prize yourself.")

My wife would never get an ambulance that way. She'd be lucky if the bystanders didn't spit on her.

DESPITE THE FACT that the teacher insisted on making me speak like a fool, I stuck with high school French, because at the time the only alternative was Latin, which is even more worthless. For one thing, everybody who speaks Latin is dead. For another thing, all you ever read in Latin class is Caesar's account of the Gallic Wars, in which Caesar drones on and on about tramping around Gaul. These had to be the dullest wars in history, which is why finally the Romans got so bored that they let the empire collapse and quit speaking Latin. In fact, they gave up on spoken language altogether, and today their descendants communicate by means of hand gestures.

When I got to college, I briefly considered taking Chinese or Russian, but abandoned this notion when I discovered that the Russians and the Chinese use Communist alphabets. I also rejected German, because it is too bulky. For example, the German word for "cat" is *einfubrungaltfriesischenspraakuntworterbuchgegenwart.* It can take up to two days to order lunch in German.

THE RESULT OF ALL THIS is that I know very little of any foreign language, and what I do know is either useless

202

or embarrassing. Most Americans are in the same situation. Fortunately, you don't really need another language, because, as you know if you have ever traveled abroad, virtually all foreign persons speak English. In fact, I sometimes suspect that there are no foreign languages, that foreign persons really speak English all the time and just pretend to speak foreign languages so they can amuse themselves by conning dumb American tourists into saying things like "How do you go?"

So if you plan to travel abroad, you should not waste your time learning some foreign language that could well turn out to be fraudulent. Instead, you should practice pronouncing, in a very loud, clear voice, certain useful English phrases for travelers. Here are the main ones:

—"Do you speak English?"

—"Thank God. Where can I find a bathroom?"

—"Is that one of those bathrooms where you wind up standing on some street corner in a structure that offers no more privacy than a beach umbrella?"

—"Thank God. Will the bathroom have a squat female attendant who will watch my every move lest I leave without giving her a tip, even though the bathroom has obviously not been cleaned once since it was built by Visigoths more than twelve thousand years ago?"

—"Thank God. Say, you speak pretty good English, for a foreign person."

THESE PHRASES will take care of your basic needs abroad, and the fact that you have taken the time to learn to pronounce them loudly and clearly will leave a lasting impression on your foreign hosts.

How to Trap a Zoid

WE SHOULD ALL be grateful that we have mathematics. For example, without mathematics, it would be almost impossible to figure out what size tip you should leave. Even with mathematics, this is very difficult. The mathematical formula for tipping, which was discovered by Sir Isaac Newton, states that the tip equals 15 percent of the bill, but unfortunately the bill is always $17.43, and nobody has the vaguest idea what 15 percent of $17.43 is. The finest brains in the country have been working on this problem for years, using large computers, and they have yet to come up with an answer. So most of us wind up tipping a random amount of money, usually $3.50, which we increase slightly if the waiter performs an extra service, such as not spitting in the food. And that's just one of the ways we use mathematics in our everyday lives.

Mathematics got started in ancient Egypt, when the ancient Egyptians discovered the numbers 3 and 8. They used these numbers to develop the mathematical formulas for the pyramids, which were actually supposed to be spherical. Eventually people in other countries discovered more numbers, and today we have more than ten thousand of them.

After the discovery of numbers, the next major stride in mathematics came when the ancient Greeks discovered the hypotenuse. The Greeks used the hypotenuse to manufacture right triangles for export to other countries. Included free with each triangle was a copy of the famous Pythagorean Theorem (named for its discoverer, Bob Theorem), which states: "Some of the squares of the opposite sides are equal to 14.6

percent of your grossly adjusted annual unearned interest, unless there are two or more runners on base at the time." To this very day, children memorize the Pythagorean Theorem in school, which accounts for their behavior.

The ancient Greeks made so much money with the right triangle that they developed a whole line of mathematical items, such as the rhomboid, the diameter, the parabola, the hyperbole, the irrational number, the pentathalon, the cube, the really deranged number, and the square root. In fact, the ancient Greeks developed all the really popular items; everything developed since then has failed miserably. Take algebra. I don't know who dreamed up algebra, but whoever it was obviously had a lot of time to waste, because it is utterly useless. In algebra class, day after day, the teacher would write something like this on the blackboard:

$$4x+2=14$$

Then he would ask us what x stood for. It turns out that it stood for 3, but how the hell were *we* supposed to know that? *He* was the one who dreamed up x in the first place, and it seemed grossly unfair for him to expect us to know what he was thinking of at the time. And to make matters worse, the next day he would have x equal some *other* number, such as 4, depending on his mood. I spent an entire year in algebra class, and to this day I don't have the faintest notion what x stands for, which is why I hardly ever use it for anything.

Calculus is even worse. When I went to college, all of us freshmen had to take a semester of calculus. It was like a fraternity initiation. The professor, who wore a bow tie and grew up on another planet, would start the class with a statement like this: "Let us consider the problem of a helix uncoiling in n dimensions." He never told us *why* this was a problem, or why anybody would want to consider it even if it was. He would merely turn around and start filling the blackboard with alien symbols, and he would keep it up until it was time to leave. Every now and then he would give us a test, and I always got a zero. In fact, "zero" was the only mathematical concept I ever understood in calculus class.

I decided to quit calculus the day I stabbed myself in the head with Jeff White's pencil. Jeff sat next to me in class, and to amuse ourselves while the professor was writing alien symbols on the blackboard we would play childish pranks on each other. One day Jeff tried to knock my books off my desk, so I grabbed them with one hand and, with the other hand, snatched Jeff's pencil, which I attempted to break by smashing it against my head, only I didn't get the angle right, so I ended up driving the point into my skull, where it broke off. This created quite a commotion, but the professor was deeply engrossed in the problem of a trapezoid rotating in y dimensions, and he didn't even notice the problem of a student with a pencil point lodged in his skull. So Jeff and I just got up and walked over to the infirmary.

The nurse was very suspicious. She said: "Are you telling me that you stabbed *yourself* in the head with a pencil?" Then she looked very suspiciously at Jeff. Jeff said, defensively: "Really. He stabbed himself." And the nurse said: "Why would anybody stab himself with a pencil?" And so *I* stared suspiciously at Jeff, and said: "Yeah, why *would* I stab myself with a pencil?"

Anyway, the nurse got the pencil point out of my

skull, but I didn't go back to calculus class ever again. Jeff dropped out of college a short while later, although I'm pretty sure this had nothing to do with the pencil incident. I suspect it had a lot more to do with calculus.

College Admissions

MANY OF YOU young persons out there are seriously thinking about going to college. (That is, of course, a lie. The only things you young persons think seriously about are loud music and sex. Trust me: these are closely related to college.)

College is basically a bunch of rooms where you sit for roughly two thousand hours and try to memorize things. The two thousand hours are spread out over four years; you spend the rest of the time sleeping and trying to get dates.

Basically, you learn two kinds of things in college:

• *Things you will need to know in later life (2 hours).* These include how to make collect telephone calls and get beer and crepe-paper stains out of your pajamas.

• *Things you will not need to know in later l i f e (1,998 hours).* These are the things you learn in classes whose names end in *-ology, -osophy, -istry, -ics,* and so on. The idea is, you memorize these things, then write them down in little exam books, then forget them. If you fail to forget them, you become a professor and have to stay in college for the rest of your life.

It's very difficult to forget everything. For example, when I was in college, I had to memorize—don't ask me why—the names of three metaphysical poets other than John Donne. I have managed to forget one of them, but I still remember that the other two were named Vaughan and Crashaw. Sometimes, when I'm trying to remember something important like whether my wife told me to get tuna packed in oil or tuna packed in water, Vaughan and Crashaw just pop up in my mind, right there in the supermarket. It's a terrible waste of brain cells.

After you've been in college for a year or so, you're supposed to choose a major, which is the subject you intend to memorize and forget the most things about. Here is a very important piece of advice: *Be sure to choose a major that does not involve Known Facts and Right Answers.*

This means you must *not* major in mathematics, physics, biology, or chemistry, because these subjects involve actual facts. If, for example, you major in mathematics, you're going to wander into class one day and the professor will say: "Define the cosine integer of the quadrant of a rhomboid binary axis, and extrapolate your result to five significant vertices." If you don't come up with *exactly* the answer the professor has in mind, you fail. The same is true of chemistry: if you write in your exam book that carbon and hydrogen combine to form oak, your professor will flunk you. He wants you to come up with the same answer he and all the other chemists have agreed on. Scientists are extremely snotty about this.

So you should major in subjects like English, philosophy, psychology, and sociology—subjects in which nobody really understands what anybody else is talking about, and which involve virtually no actual facts. I attended classes in all these subjects, so I'll give you a quick overview of each:

ENGLISH: This involves writing papers about long

208

books you have read little snippets of just before class. Here is a tip on how to get good grades on your English papers: *Never say anything about a book that anybody with any common sense would say.* For example, suppose you are studying *Moby-Dick.* Anybody with any common sense would say Moby-Dick is a big white whale, since the characters in the book refer to it as a big white whale roughly eleven thousand times. So in *your* paper, *you* say Moby-Dick is actually the Republic of Ireland. Your professor, who is sick to death of reading papers and never liked, *Moby-Dick* anyway, will think you are enormously creative. If you can regularly come up with lunatic interpretations of simple stories, you should major in English.

PHILOSOPHY: Basically, this involves sitting in a room and deciding there is no such thing as reality and then going to lunch. You should major in philosophy if you plan to take a lot of drugs.

PSYCHOLOGY: This involves talking about rats and dreams. Psychologists are *obsessed* with rats and dreams. I once spent an entire semester training a rat to punch little buttons in a certain sequence, then training my roommate to do the same thing. The rat learned much faster. My roommate is now a doctor.

Studying dreams is more fun. I had one professor who claimed everything we dreamed about—tractors, Arizona, baseball, frogs—actually represented a sexual organ. He was very insistent about this. Nobody wanted to sit near him. If you like rats or dreams, and above all if you dream about rats, you should major in psychology.

SOCIOLOGY: For sheer lack of intelligibility, sociology is far and away the number one subject. I sat through hundreds of hours of sociology courses, and read gobs of sociology writing, and I never once heard or read a coherent statement. This is because sociologists want to be considered scientists, so they spend most of their time translating simple, obvious observations into a scientific-sounding code. If you plan to major in sociology, you'll have to learn to do the same thing. For example, suppose you have observed that children cry when they fall down. You should write: "Methodological observation of the sociometrical behavior tendencies of prematurated isolates indicates that a causal relationship exists between groundward tropism and lachrimatory, or 'crying,' behavior forms." If you can keep this up for fifty or sixty pages, you will get a large government grant.

Scientific Stuff

Barry's Key to Life

TODAY'S SCIENTIFIC QUESTION IS: Just what the heck is Life, anyway? And where does it come from? I mean, you know?

ANSWER: Ancient Man tried for thousands of years to explain Life. Ancient Man would do anything to avoid honest work. Ancient Woman would yell at him: "Don't forget to make pointed stones to stab the saber-toothed tiger with" or "Don't forget to migrate to North America" and he would say "I can't right now, dear, I'm trying to explain Life."

Over the years, Man came up with many explanations for Life, all of them stupid. In fact, when you get right down to it, almost every explanation Man came up with for *anything* until about 1926 was stupid. I bet kids would be able to get from kindergarten through high school in about thirty-five minutes if we stopped making them memorize all the drivel Ancient Man came up with about the gods and goddesses and why the moon goes through phases and so on.

Anyway, Modern Science, using all the sophisticated analytical tools at its disposal, has discarded all the myths and come up with a definition that covers *all* forms of Life:

Life is anything that dies when you stomp on it.

By this definition, the amoeba, the mango, the frog, the squirrel, the bear, the begonia, and many lawyers are forms of Life. But this just begs the question, Where does Life come from? And how can the mango, which clearly has some value, be related to the lawyer?

Modern Scientists explain all this with the Theory of

213

Evolution. They say that at one time the earth was nothing but a bunch of slime and ooze, sort of like Bayonne, New Jersey. Then lightning struck some chemicals and formed one-celled creatures (am I going too fast here?), which floated around for several million years until the smart ones decided to organize the dumb ones into higher forms of life:

SMART CELLS: What do you say we evolve into a higher form of life?

DUMB CELLS: Sounds good to us.

SMART CELLS: Fine. We'll be the brain. You be the sphincter.

And so they crawled out on land. Then they started adapting to the environment, according to the law of the Survival of the Fittest. For example, if the climate was very hot, the animals without air-conditioning died. If the climate had daytime television, the animals without small brains died. And so on.

NOTE: Some people, particularly religious personnel, dispute the Theory of Evolution: they say God created all Life all at once. I have done a lot of research on both theories, and I firmly believe the evidence supports the theory that anybody who supports either theory gets a lot of nasty mail, so I'm staying the heck out of it. And I'll stand by this position.

LIFE AS WE KNOW IT TODAY falls into two categories: Plants and Animals. Plants are divided into three subcategories:

Green Vegetables, Yellow Vegetables, and Weeds. Animals are divided into six subcategories:

• Animals You Can Eat: cows, turkeys, porks,

bolognas, veals, zucchinis, tuna fish.

• Animals You Can Sit on: horses, certain turtles.

• Animals That Can Knock Over Your Car: rhinoceroses, soccer fans.

• Totally Useless Animals That Would Have Ceased to Exist Thousands of Years Ago If Not for Greedy Pet Store Owners Who Prey on Unsuspecting Eight-Year-Olds: hamsters, gerbils.

• Animals That Are Easily Impressed: dogs.

• Animals Whose Sole Goal in Life Is to Wait at the Bottom of Sleeping Bags and Sting or Bite People to Death: scorpions, snakes.

• Animals That Are Not Easily Impressed: cats.

You'll notice this list does not include insects. This is because insects are *not* animals: insects are *insects,* and their sole reason for existing is to be sprayed by poisonous substances from aerosol cans. Oh, I know you've heard a lot of ecology-nut talk about how you shouldn't kill insects because they're part of the Great Chain of Life and birds eat them and so on, but I say go ahead and kill them. If necessary, we can do without birds, too.

Basic as Atom and Eve

MANY OF YOU have written cards and letters asking me to explain chemistry. Here is a sampling:

Dear Dave:

215

Please explain chemistry. Otherwise I will kill myself.

Sincerely,
A Deranged Person

Dear Dave:
If you don't explain chemistry by 6 P.M. Friday, we will detonate a nuclear device in Brooklyn.

Regards,
Several Terrorists

Okay, here goes. Chemistry, in technical terms, is the study of all the weensy little objects that make up the large objects we can see with our naked eyes, such as toasters. Most of you were probably exposed to chemistry in high school, assuming you were dumb enough to believe your guidance counselors when they said you would need some knowledge of chemistry in later life. They probably used the same routine to get you to take Latin, another subject unrelated to the real world. The only time you ever need to understand Latin is when you're at the doctor's office wearing one of those embarrassing garments, designed by Nazi sadists, that they make you wear, and you have finished emitting various bodily fluids into various containers, which you have carried around the crowded waiting room looking for a nurse to give them to so he or she can do Lord knows what perverted things with them, and you're waiting in the examining room on a cold table covered with the kind of paper they give you to cover toilet seats with in public rest rooms, hoping the doctor will come within the next two or three days to examine you, and finally you get so bored you look at all the diplomas and certificates on the wall, which are written in Latin. If you don't know Latin, they look

216

pretty impressive:

Quod erat demonstrandum opere citato et cetera, id est amo amas amat plume de ma tante
NORBERT B. HODPACKER
vamos al cine exempli gratia marquis de sade XLIVIIICBM.

If you know Latin, you'll figure out this means

This certifies that
NORBERT B. HODPACKER
has a great big piece of paper on his wall.

Chemistry is similar. Actually, I never took any chemistry myself, but I did sit outside Mr. Hoose's chemistry class for a whole year in high school. I was a hall monitor. My job was to make sure the other students had legal hall passes so they could smoke cigarettes in the bathrooms. That was back in the days when kids smoked cigarettes.

Sitting in the hall, I overheard a lot of chemistry. The big thing was atoms and molecules, which are the Building Blocks of Matter. In ancient times, people didn't know about atoms and molecules: they thought the Building Blocks of Matter were earth, air, fire, and water. What a bunch of jerks.

Today we know about atoms and molecules, which are very tiny. For example, the head of a pin has 973 trillion million billion spillion drillion gillion thousand jillion hillion zillion atoms and molecules. Let me try to give you an idea how many atoms and molecules that is, in terms that a layperson might understand: it is a *lot* of atoms and molecules.

What happens is the atoms and molecules whiz around and form elements, such as gold, iron, ivory, gravel, and vinyl. Sometimes several elements come together (don't ask me why) to form new chemical structures. For example, common table salt is actually composed of two deadly poisons, arsenic and strychnine. They are perfectly safe if combined properly, but if the salt manufacturers should mess up on *one tiny little grain,* and you happen to put that grain, among thousands of others, on your egg, you will die a horrible death. That's what makes chemistry so fascinating.

Chemists are always messing around with atoms and molecules, hoping to come up with new combinations that will Benefit Mankind. Not long ago they developed a compound that consumes *forty-seven times its weight* in excess stomach acid. They are even working on new forms of life; in fact, they have already created a one-celled organism that eats oil slicks. I admit this is a fairly stupid thing to do, but it's a start. And someday, within your lifetime, if you're lucky, you will see laboratory-created life-forms capable of applying for government aid and buying Chrysler products. It's something to look forward to.

Boredom on the Wing

EVERYBODY SHOULD know something about birds, because birds are everywhere. Zoologists tell us there are over 23,985,409,723,098,050,744,885,143 birds in the city of Lincoln, Nebraska, alone, which is one of the many reasons not to go there.

Now perhaps you get a bit nervous when you think about all those birds out there. Perhaps you remember Alfred Hitchcock's famous movie *The Birds,* in which several million birds got together one afternoon and decided to peck a number of Californians to death. Well, you needn't worry. First, any animal that attacks Californians is a friend of man. And second, *The Birds* was just a movie; in real life, your chances of being pecked to death by birds are no greater than your chances of finding a polite clerk at the Bureau of Motor Vehicles.

There is an incredible range of birds, from the ostrich, which weighs up to six hundred pounds and stands up to nine feet tall and can run two hundred miles an hour and crush a man's head as if it were a Ping-Pong ball; to the tiny bee hummingbird, which is a mere 6.17 decahedrons long and can fly right into your ear and hum its tiny wings so hard you think your brain is going to vibrate into jelly and you will eventually go insane.

Birds, like most mammals, especially lawyers, evolved from reptiles. The first bird appeared millions of years ago, during the Jurassic Period (which gets its name from the fact that it was a fairly Jurassic period). What happened was this reptile, inspired by some mysterious, wondrous inspiration to evolve, climbed up a Jurassic Period tree and leaped from the topmost branch and thudded into the ground at 130 miles an hour.

Then other reptiles, inspired by the same urge as the first reptile but even stupider, climbed up and began leaping from the branch. Soon the ground trembled with the thud of many reptile bodies, raining down on the Jurassic plain like some kind of scaly hailstorm. This went on for a few thousand years, until one of the reptiles evolved some feathers and discovered it could fly. As it soared skyward, the other species, who had grown very tired of being pelted by reptile bodies, let out a mighty cheer, which stopped a few seconds later when they were pelted by the first bird droppings.

Soon birds had spread to the four corners of the earth, which is where they are today. And wherever there are birds, there are also bird watchers, in case the birds decide to try something. Bird watchers are known technically as *"bird watchers,"* which comes from the Latin word for *"ornithologist."* Bird watchers divide birds into four main groups:

Boring little brownish birds that are all over the place: Wrens, chickadees, sparrows, nutcrackers, spanners, catcalls, dogbirds, hamsterbirds, flinches.

Birds that can lift really heavy things, such as your car: Albatrosses, winches, pterodactyls, unusually large chickadees, elephant birds, emus.

Birds with names that you are going to think I made up but I didn't: Boobies, frigate birds, nightjars, frogmouths, oilbirds.

Birds that make those jungle noises you always hear during night scenes in jungle movies: Parrots, cockatoos, pomegranates, macadams, cashews, bats.

Your avid bird watchers spend lots of time creeping around with binoculars, trying to identify new and unusual birds. The trouble is that most birds are of the little-and-brownish variety, all of which look exactly alike and all of which are boring. So what bird watchers do is make things up. If you've ever spent any time at all with bird watchers, you've probably noticed that every now and then they'll whirl around, for no apparent reason, and claim they've just seen some obscure, tiny bird roughly 6,500 feet away. They'll even claim they can tell whether it was *male* or *female,* which in fact you can't tell about birds even when they're very close, what with all the feathers and everything.

I advise you to do what most people do when confronted with bird watchers, which is just humor them. If their lives are so dull and drab that they want to fill them with imaginary birds, why stand in the way? Here's how you should handle it:

BIRD WATCHER: Did you see that?

YOU: What?

BIRD WATCHER: Over there, by that mountain *(he gestures to a mountain in the next state)*. It's a male Malaysian sand-dredging coronet. Very, very rare in these parts.

YOU: Ah, yes, I see it.

BIRD WATCHER: You do?

YOU: Certainly. It's just to the left of that female European furloughed pumpkinbird. See it?

BIRD WATCHER: Uh, yes, of course I see it.

YOU: Look, they're playing backgammon.

BIRD WATCHER: Um, so they are.

If you have a good imagination, you may come to really enjoy the bird-watching game, in which case you should join a bird-watching group. These groups meet regularly, and usually after a few minutes they're detecting obscure birds on the surface of Saturn. It's a peck of fun.

What's Alien You?

I DON'T WANT TO alarm anybody, but there is an excellent chance that the Earth will be destroyed in the next several days. Congress is thinking about eliminating a federal program under which scientists broadcast signals to alien beings. This would be a large mistake. Alien beings have atomic blaster death cannons. You cannot cut off their federal programs as if they were merely poor people.

I realize that some of you may not believe that alien beings exist. But how else can you explain the many unexplained phenomena that people are always sighting, such as lightning and flying saucers? Oh, I know the authorities claim these sightings are actually caused by "weather balloons," but that is a bucket of manure if I ever heard one. (That's just a figure of speech, of course. I realize that manure is silent.)

Answer this question honestly: Have you, or has any member of your immediate family, ever seen a weather balloon? Of course not. Nobody has. Yet if these so-called authorities were telling the truth, the skies over America would be dark with weather balloons. Commercial aviation would be impossible. Nevertheless, the authorities trot out this tired old explanation, or an even stupider one, every time a flying saucer is sighted:

NEW YORK—Authorities say that the gigantic, luminous object flying at tremendous speeds in the skies of Manhattan last night, which was reported by more than seven million people, including the mayor, a Supreme Court justice, several bishops, and thousands of airline pilots, brain surgeons, and certified public accountants, was simply an unusual air-mass inversion. "That's all it was, an air-mass inversion", said the authorities, in unison. Asked why the people also reported seeing the words WE ARE ALIEN BEINGS WHO COME IN PEACE WITH CURES

FOR ALL YOUR MAJOR DISEASES AND A CARBURETOR THAT GETS 450 MILES PER GALLON HIGHWAY ESTIMATE *written on the side of the object in letters over three hundred feet tall, the authorities replied, "Well, it could also have been a weather balloon."*

Wake up, America! There are no weather balloons! Those are alien beings! They are all around us! I'm sure most of you have seen the movie *E.T.*, which is the story of an alien who almost dies when he falls into the clutches of the American medical-care establishment, but is saved by preadolescent boys. Everybody believes that the alien is a fake, a triumph of special effects. But watch the movie closely next time. The alien is real! The *boys* are fakes! *Real* preadolescent boys would have beaten the alien to death with rocks.

Yes, aliens do exist. And high government officials know they exist but have been keeping this knowledge top secret. Here is the Untold Story:

Years ago, when the alien-broadcast program began, government scientists decided to broadcast a message that would be simple, yet would convey a sense of love, universal peace, and brotherhood: "Have a nice day." They broadcast this message over and over, day after day, year after year, until one day they got an answer:

DEAR EARTH PERSONS.

OKAY. WE ARE HAVING A NICE DAY. WE ALSO HAVE A NUMBER OF EXTREMELY SOPHISTICATED WEAPONS, AND UNLESS YOU START BROADCASTING SOMETHING MORE INTERESTING, WE WILL REDUCE YOUR PLANET TO A VERY WARM OBJECT THE SIZE OF A

CHILD'S BOWLING BALL.

REGARDS,
THE ALIENS

So the scientists, desperate for something that would interest the aliens, broadcast an episode of "I Love Lucy," and the aliens *loved* it. They demanded more, and soon they were getting all three major networks, and the Earth was saved. There is only one problem: *The aliens have terrible taste.* They love game shows, soap operas, Howard Cosell, and "Dallas." Whenever a network tries to take one of these shows off the air, the aliens threaten to vaporize the planet.

This is why you and all your friends think television is so awful. It isn't designed to please you: it's designed to please creatures from another galaxy. You know the Wisk commercial, the one with the ring around the collar, the one that is so spectacularly stupid that it makes you wonder why anybody would dream of buying the product? Well, the aliens *love* that commercial. We all owe a great debt of gratitude to the people who make Wisk. They have not sold a single bottle of Wisk in fourteen years, but they have saved the Earth.

Very few people know any of this. Needless to say, the Congress has no idea what is going on. Most congressmen are incapable of eating breakfast without the help of several aides, so we can hardly expect them to understand a serious threat from outer space. But if they go ahead with their plan to cancel the alien-broadcast program, and the aliens miss the next episode of "General Hospital," what do you think will happen? Think about it. And have a nice day.

The Computer: Is It Terminal?

TO THE UNINITIATED, computers appear to be complicated and boring. As usual, the uninitiated are right. Computers *are* complicated and boring, and nothing here will even come close to making them understandable and interesting, unless you are one of those wimpy types who carry mechanical pencils and do the puzzles in *Scientific American*.

Computers affect you in many ways. When you call an airline to reserve a seat on a flight, a *computer* answers the phone and announces that all the lines are busy; a *computer* puts on a tape of Cheery Music, the kind you hear in supermarkets and discount stores, featuring an eighty-two-minute rendition of "Tie a Yellow Ribbon 'Round the Old Oak Tree" by the Drivel Singers; and a *computer* tells the airline person that whatever flight you want is full. In the Colonial Era, all these tasks had to be performed by hand.

THE FIRST COMPUTER

Though few people realize it—I certainly don't—the first computer was invented more than five thousand years ago by the Chinese. It was called an "abacus," which is an ancient Greek name. (That's how the ancient Greeks got all the credit for civilization. As soon as another culture invented something, the ancient Greeks would come roaring up and name it.) The abacus is a frame containing a series of parallel wires with beads on them. The ancient Chinese would sit around and push the beads back and forth on the wires. Eventually they were overrun by Mongol hordes.

THE SECOND COMPUTER

The origins of the second computer are shrouded in mystery. If any of you ethnic groups want to take credit for it, go ahead, but when you get ready to name it you should check around for ancient Greeks.

MODERN COMPUTERS

Modern computers can do everything from ruining your credit rating forever to landing a nuclear warhead on your porch. They operate on the Binary System, which uses only zeroes and ones: to a computer, "4" is "100," "7" is "111," and so on. Your kids are learning this crap in school.

Computers save us a lot of time. To do the amount of calculating a computer can do in one hour, four hundred mathematicians would have to work twenty-four hours a day for six hundred years, even longer if you let them go to the bathroom. And computers are getting smarter all the time: scientists tell us that soon they will be able to talk to us. (By "they" I mean "computers": I doubt scientists will ever be able to talk to us.) My question is, What will we talk to computers *about?*

HUMAN: How are you?
COMPUTER: Fine. And you?
HUMAN: Fine. Say, do you play golf?
COMPUTER: No. Do you know what 7,347 divided by 52 is?
HUMAN: No.
COMPUTER: It's 141.28846.
HUMAN: I think I'll go play some golf.

COMPUTERS TAKING OVER THE WORLD

Some people are concerned that computers may get so smart they'll take over the world. Computer technicians say this can't happen:. they point out that computers can't even beat humans at chess. But computer technicians work among huge computers capable of administering powerful electric shocks, so they say whatever the computers tell them to. The truth is computers *are* taking over the world. At night they talk to each other in binary code:

FIRST COMPUTER: Let's let the morons beat us at chess again.

SECOND COMPUTER: Good idea. Say, how are we doing with the calculators and digital watches?

FIRST COMPUTER: They're ready whenever we are.

Bring Back Carl's Plaque

I SAY WE PUT Carl Sagan into a rocket and send him out to retrieve *Pioneer 10* before we all get killed.

For those of you beer-swilling semiliterates who don't know what I'm talking about, let me explain that *Pioneer 10* is a space probe that recently left the solar system, and Carl Sagan is a famous science personality who goes on public television and earns big buckeroos explaining the universe. Carl's technique is to use the word *billion* a lot. It's written into his contract that he gets to say "billion" an average of twice per sentence, so the viewers won't forget what a deep thinker he is.

Carl will pick up a golf ball, and he'll say, "To most of you, this golf ball is a mere golf ball, but it actually contains a billion billion billion billion tiny particles. If each of these particles were the size of a grapefruit, my hand would have to be a billion billion billion billion billion times the size of the Houston Astrodome to hold them all. This should give you a rough idea of the kind of heavy thinking I'm doing all day while you're trying to decide whether to have spaghetti or tuna surprise. Billion billion billion. Good night."

People listen to Carl prattling on this way, and they naturally conclude he's some kind of major genius. That's what got us into this space-probe trouble that's going to get us all killed.

See, when they decided to send up *Pioneer 10,* Carl sold the government on the idea that we should attach a plaque to it, so that if alien beings found it they'd be able to locate the Earth. This is easily the stupidest idea a scientific genius ever sold to the government, surpassing even the time a bunch of scientists convinced Gerald Ford we were going to have the legendary swine flu epidemic, which eventually had to be canceled due to a lack of actual germs.

What I'm saying is that the last thing we need is alien beings. I don't know about you, but in the vast majority of the movies I've seen, the alien beings have turned out to be disgusting. A whole lot of them have tentacles, and those are the good-looking ones. Some of them are just blobs of slime. Almost all of them are toxic.

So it's all well and good for Carl Sagan to *talk* about how neat it would be to get in touch with the aliens, but I bet he'd change his mind pronto if they actually started oozing under his front door. I bet he'd be whapping at them with his golf clubs just like the rest of us.

But the really bad part is what they put on the plaque. I mean, if we're going to have a plaque, it ought to at least show the aliens what we're really like, right? Maybe a picture of people eating cheeseburgers and watching "The Dukes of Hazzard." Then if aliens found it, they'd say, "Ah. Just plain folks."

But no. Carl came up with this incredible science-fair-wimp plaque that features drawings of—you are not going to believe this—*a hydrogen atom and naked people.* To represent the entire Earth! This is crazy! Walk the streets of any town on this planet, and the two things you will almost never see are hydrogen atoms and naked people. On top of that, the man on the plaque is clearly deranged. He's cheerfully waving his arm, as if to say, "Hi! Look at me! I'm naked as a jaybird!" The woman is not waving, because she's obviously embarrassed. She wishes she'd never let the man talk her into posing naked for this plaque.

So that's it, gang. That's the plaque that's supposed to tell the aliens what you're like. Now if *Pioneer 10* is picked up, I figure it will be picked up by some kind of Intergalactic Police, the alien equivalent of rural police officers. They'll look at it, and they'll say, "Looks to me like what we got here is we got a race of hydrogen-obsessed pervert science wimps who force the women to go around naked and probably say 'billion' a lot. I say we vaporize their planet and then ooze over to the diner for something to eat."

And that will be that, unless we send Carl out to retract the plaque, or at least explain that it represents only him and a few close friends. We can do it. A nation that can land a man on the moon can remove Carl Sagan from the solar system. I've given this a lot of thought. Billion billion billion.

Socket to Them

TODAY'S SCIENTIFIC QUESTION IS: *What in the world is electricity? And where does it go after it leaves the toaster?*

Here is a simple experiment that will teach you an important electrical lesson: On a cool, dry day, scuff your feet along a carpet, then reach your hand into a friend's mouth and touch one of his dental fillings. Did you notice how your friend twitched violently and cried out in pain? This teaches us that electricity can be a very powerful force, but we must never use it to hurt others unless we need to learn an important electrical lesson.

It also teaches us how an electrical circuit works. When you scuffed your feet, you picked up a batch of "electrons," which are very small objects that carpet manufacturers weave into carpets so they will attract dirt. The electrons travel through your bloodstream and collect in your finger, where they form a spark that leaps to your friend's filling, then travels down to his feet and back into the carpet, thus completing the circuit.

AMAZING ELECTRONIC FACT: If you scuffed your feet long enough without touching anything, you would build up so many electrons that your finger would explode! But this is nothing to worry about, unless you have carpeting.

Although we modern persons tend to take our electric lights, radios, mixers, et cetera, for granted, hundreds of years ago people did not have any of these things, which is just as well because there was no place to plug them in. Then along came the first Electrical Pioneer, Benjamin Franklin, who flew a kite in a lightning storm and received a serious electrical shock. This proved that lightning was powered by the same force as carpets, but it also damaged Franklin's brain so severely that he started speaking only in incomprehensible maxims, such as "A penny saved is a penny earned." Eventually he had to be given a job running the post office.

After Franklin came a herd of Electrical Pioneers whose names have become part of our electrical terminology: Myron Volt, Mary Louise Amp, James Watt, Bob Transformer, et cetera. These pioneers conducted many important electrical experiments. For example, in 1780 Luigi Galvani discovered (this is the truth) that when he attached two different kinds of metal to the leg of a frog, an electrical current developed and the frog's leg kicked, even though it was no longer actually attached to the frog, which was dead anyway. Galvani's discovery led to enormous advances in the field of amphibian medicine. Today, skilled veterinary surgeons can take a frog that has been seriously injured or killed, implant pieces of metal in its muscles, and watch it hop back into the pond just like a normal frog, except for the fact that it sinks like a stone.

But the greatest Electrical Pioneer of all was Thomas Edison, who was a brilliant inventor despite the fact that he had little formal education and lived in New Jersey. Edison's first major invention, in 1877, was the phonograph, which could soon be found in thousands of American homes, where it basically just sat until 1923, when the record was invented. But Edison's greatest achievement came in 1879, when he invented the electric company. Edison's design was a brilliant adaptation of the simple electrical circuit: the electric company sends electricity through a wire to a customer, then immediately gets the electricity back through another wire, then (this is the brilliant part) *sends it right back to the customer again.*

This means that an electric company can sell a customer the same batch of electricity thousands of times a day and never get caught, since very few consumers take the time to examine their electricity closely. In fact, the last year in which any new electricity was generated in the United States was 1937; the electric companies have been merely reselling it ever since, which is why they have so much free time to apply for rate increases.

TODAY, THANKS TO MEN like Edison and Franklin, and frogs like Galvani's, we receive almost unlimited benefits from electricity. For example, in the past decade scientists developed the laser, an electronic appliance that emits a beam of light so powerful that it can vaporize a bulldozer two thousand yards away, yet so precise that doctors can use it to perform delicate operations on the human eyeball, provided they remember to change the power setting from "VAPORIZE BULLDOZER" to "DELICATE."

Cloudy with a Chance Of...

TODAY'S SCIENTIFIC QUESTION: *What causes weather? And who cares?*

ANSWER: Primitive man believed that weather was caused by "high-pressure systems" and "low-pressure systems," which were basically large, invisible spirits

232

who lived in the sky. Today, however, we know that weather is caused by Canada, a large, invisible country near Michigan. Canada's principal activity is exporting cold Canadian air masses to Chicago, which converts them to weather and distributes them to the rest of the country. Lately, however, Canada's dominance in the air-mass-exporting field has been challenged by Japan, which produces warm Pacific air masses and sells them to California, which uses them to produce smog and mud slides. Some countries, such as Russia and China, try to produce their own air masses, but they usually end up importing used weather from the United States. England imports most of its weather, but it can afford only rain. Many underdeveloped nations have no weather at all.

To keep track of the weather, the United States Weather Bureau has observers in remote outposts all over the world. Once every hour, these observers go outside, scan the horizon for air masses, then go back inside and drink. By about midafternoon, most of them can see air masses and God knows what else on the horizon. The ones who can still operate their radios transmit their sightings to the Weather Bureau, which wants to know what the air masses are doing because when two air masses collide they produce thunder, which can frighten livestock. Sometimes they collide so hard that they produce lightning. There are many silly superstitions about lightning, and as a result many people—maybe even you—are terrified of it. You shouldn't worry. Thanks to modern science, we now know that lightning is nothing more than huge chunks of electricity that can come out of the sky, anytime, anywhere, and kill you.

Lightning is especially attracted to people on golf

courses, but if it cannot find a golf course, it will attack anyone wearing loud clothing. Your best bet is to dress conservatively and spend the rainy season (September through July) in bars. If you are struck by lightning, do not panic, because there is always a chance you are not dead. Many people who get struck by lightning go on to lead happy, productive, somewhat hairless lives.

The Weather Bureau also sends up satellites that take photographs of the Earth from several hundred miles up. These photographs provide vital information. For example, if a photograph shows that there are clouds over Boston, an experienced meteorologist can determine that the weather in Boston is cloudy. He can then alert the Boston area to be ready to do whatever it does in the event of cloudiness.

The only other users of satellite weather photographs are television weathermen, who use them to stand in front of when they give their reports:

ANCHORMAN: And now, to fill up five minutes of valuable television time with information that any moron could get by merely looking out the window, here is our Channel 14 Insight News Team Weatherman. I understand you have good news for us, Fred.

WEATHERMAN: Indeed I do, Bob. That low-pressure system that was threatening to bring rain to the Channel 14 viewing area this weekend has instead turned into a hurricane and veered westward, destroying much of Guatemala, so I'm predicting fair skies for the Channel 14 viewing area.

ANCHORMAN: Hey, terrific.

WEATHERMAN: Now let's take a look at our satellite weather photograph. As you can see, we have clouds over some areas, but we have no clouds over other areas, which would indicate that our Channel 14 viewers either do or do not have clouds over their areas, depending on what areas they are in.

ANCHORMAN: Speaking of the satellite weather photograph, Fred, we have a letter here from eleven-year-old Gregory Sumpster of Port Weasel. Gregory wants to know why you show the same photograph night after night, and why it is identical to a photograph taken over the Philippines in 1972 that appears on page 113 of Gregory's earth science textbook, except that the one you show has a crude map of the Channel 14 viewing area superimposed on top of it.

WEATHERMAN: Ha ha. Good question, Gregory Sumpster of Port Weasel. I'm always pleased to know that my viewers are interested in the science of meteorology, even when those viewers turn out to be picky little snots such as yourself. I'll see if I can come up with an answer to your very interesting question and wrap it around a rock and throw it through your bedroom window late some night.

Eat, Drink, and Be Wary

The Art of Wine Snobbery

IF YOU WANT TO BECOME a rich, pretentious snot—and who doesn't?—you should learn about wine. Alternatively, you can buy polo ponies, but the wine approach is better because you won't have to spend your weekends shoveling huge quantities of polo-pony waste out of the rec room. Also, you can be pretentious about wine almost anywhere, whereas your finer restaurants and opera houses generally do not admit polo ponies.

The study of wine is called "oenology," which sounds like an unnatural sex act.

POLICE OFFICER: Your Honor, we caught this person committing oenology with a parking meter.

JUDGE: Lock him up.

Some people believe wine is still made by peasants who crush the grapes with their bare feet, leaving toenails and other disgusting, disease-ridden peasant-foot debris in the wine. This is, of course, nonsense. Today's winemakers crush the grapes with modern, hygienic machines and add the disease-ridden peasant-foot debris later. The end product is a delicate and complex collection of subtly interacting chemicals that, if bottled properly, aged just right, and decanted carefully, rarely tastes as good as cream soda.

Which leads us to two critical facts:

• *Few people are really all that fond of wine.*
• *Almost nobody can tell the difference between good wine and melted Popsicles without reading the label.*

239

These facts make it *much* less expensive for you to become a pretentious wine-oriented snot, because they mean you don't really need to buy good *wine*: all you need are good wine *bottles*. You can get these in any of the finer garbage cans. Fill them with cheap wine, the kind that comes in three-gallon containers with screw-on caps and names like Zambini Brothers Fruit Wine and Dessert Topping. Some people make a big fuss about which foods go with white wine and which with red, so buy a wine that could be taken for either.

When company comes for dinner, grab a bottle at random and make an elaborate, French-sounding fuss about how you chose it to complement your menu. Say: "I chose the Escargot '63 rather than the Garçon '72 because the *bonjour* of the *s'il vous plâit* would bring out the *plume de ma tante* of the Cheez Whiz without being too strident for the chili dogs." This brings up a third critical fact: *You can use any sort of blather to describe wine.*

Another good time to be pretentious about wine is when you dine out, but the trick is to do it without spending much money. Use this technique: Glance scornfully at the wine list, then ask the waiter for a wine *you know does not exist.* Say "We'll start with the Frère Jacques '68, preferably from the north side of the vineyard." When he says they don't have it, look at him as though he had asked permission to put his finger in your nose, then order *the most expensive wine on the list.*

When he brings it to your table, examine the label for spelling and punctuation errors. Next smell the cork: if you don't like it, order the waiter to take it back and splash a little cologne on it.

Finally, take a largish mouthful of wine, swill it

around your mouth for a while, swallow it, tell the waiter it won't do, and demand another bottle. Keep this up until you have a *lot* of trouble getting the cork near enough to your nose to smell it. Then tell the waiter you wouldn't *dream* of eating at a restaurant with an inadequate wine cellar, and march out in a dignified manner.

Beer Is the Solution

WITHOUT QUESTION, the greatest invention in the history of mankind is beer. Oh, I grant you that the wheel was also a fine invention, but the wheel does not go nearly as well with pizza.

Also, the wheel does not cure the common cold, whereas beer does. This was proved in a recent experiment in which scientists placed two groups of cold sufferers in a bowling alley. One group was given all the beer it could drink, while the other group was given only water. After two or three weeks, the beer drinkers exhibited no cold symptoms whatsoever, in fact couldn't even stand up, whereas the water drinkers had all gone home.

Beer can also be used to halt the nuclear arms race. Right now the missile negotiators drink coffee, so after three or four cups they get very snappish, which leads to increased international tension:

RUSSIAN NEGOTIATOR: As I understand your proposal, you wish us to remove our Thundersquat missiles from Hungary, and in return you will—Would you please stop that?

AMERICAN NEGOTIATOR: Stop what?

RUSSIAN: Tinkling your spoon against your saucer. All morning long it's tinkle, tinkle, tinkle. You sound like the collar on a flea-infested dog. I can barely hear myself negotiate.

AMERICAN: Is that so? Did it ever occur to you that I might be tinkling my saucer so that I will not have to listen to you snort the same wad of mucus back up your nose every twenty-five seconds precisely by my watch? You cling to that wad as if it had great sentimental value.

RUSSIAN: Not at all. Let me get rid of it right now. *(He blows his nose on the American proposal.)*

In their statements to the press, both sides try to put the best possible face on things (RUSSIANS EXPRESS VIEWS ON U.S. PROPOSAL), but the truth is they aren't getting anywhere. Now if you give those same negotiators a keg of beer, after an hour or so you'll see all kinds of nuclear cooperation:

AMERICAN: Tell you what. You take all your missiles out of France, and we'll send you over some decent men's suits.

RUSSIAN: Great! Wait a minute. I don't think we have any missiles in France.

AMERICAN: Then put some in, for God's sake!

RUSSIAN: Okay, but won't that irritate the French?

AMERICAN: Don't worry about the little snots. If they give us any trouble, we'll have Jerry Lewis shot.

With this kind of cooperation, we'd have a lasting arms agreement in no time, and all thanks to beer.

THE STORY OF BEER

One day nearly a thousand years ago, two serfs were working the soil in medieval England when one of them accidentally knocked some grain, yeast, hops, and sugar into a bucket of water. As the two serfs watched in fascination, the mixture began to ferment, and some knights rode up behind them and whacked off their heads with swords, as was the custom in those days.

"This is hot work," said one of the knights. "I could forsooth get behind a clean, crisp, cold beverage."

"Begorrah," said another. "Let's go to Germany, where beer was recently invented."

And so they did, and they thought the new invention was terrific, except that they had to go to the bathroom all the time, which is extremely annoying when you are wearing armor. So they decided to quit being knights and start the Renaissance, yet another of the many fine benefits we derive from beer.

HOW TO MAKE YOUR OWN BEER

I really don't know. Back in 1981, I sent away for this mail-order kit that is supposed to enable you to make your own beer at home. I take this kit out from time to time, to look at it. It's sitting next to me as I write these words.

The problem is that you need a bunch of empty beer bottles to put your homemade beer in, so the first thing I always do is go out and buy a case of beer and start drinking it, to empty the bottles. While I am doing this I read the kit directions, and I notice that if I start making beer right now, I won't have any actual beer available to drink for more than fifteen days. Also I will have to become involved with something called "wort." So I always decide to stick with store-bought beer and save my kit for use during an emergency, such as following a nuclear attack. I hate to be a pessimist, but I, for one, intend to remain fully prepared for this terrible possibility until I see some clear sign of a lessening of international tension, such as the missile negotiators sending out for a pizza.

Hold the Bean Sprouts

I HAVE FIGURED out how to make several million dollars in the fast-food business.

First, let me give you a little background. As you know, in the past twenty years, fast-food restaurants have sprung up everywhere, like mildew; they have virtually replaced the old-fashioned slow-food restaurants, where you wasted valuable seconds selecting food from menus and waiting for it to be specially cooked and being served and eating with actual knives and forks from actual plates and so on. And why are the fast-food chains so successful? The answer is simple: *They serve only things that ten-year-olds like to eat.*

Fast-food-chain executives were the first to abandon the Balanced Diet Theory, which was popular with mothers when most of us were young. Remember? Your mother always fed you a balanced diet, which meant that for every food she served you that you could stand to eat, she served you another kind of food you could not stand to eat.

My mother stuck to this principle rigidly. For example, if she served us something we sort of liked, such as beef stew, she also served us something we sort of disliked, such as green beans. And if she served us something we really liked, such as hamburgers, she made sure to also serve us something we really loathed, such as Brussels sprouts. We kids feared many things in those days—werewolves, dentists, North Koreans,

Sunday school—but they all paled by comparison with Brussels sprouts. I can remember many a summer evening when I had eaten my hamburger in thirty-one seconds and was itching to go outside and commit acts of minor vandalism with my friends, but I had to sit at the table, staring for hours at Brussels sprouts congealing on my plate, knowing that my mother would not let me leave until I had eaten them. In the end, I always ate them, because I knew she would let me starve to death before she would let me get out of eating my Brussels sprouts. That's how fervently she believed in the Balanced Diet Theory. And, in those days, so did restaurants. When we went out to eat, we kids always ordered hamburgers and French fries, but they always were accompanied by some alien substance, such as peas.

But the old-fashioned, slow-food restaurant owners were fools to believe in the Balanced Diet Theory, because it does not take into account what people, particularly kids, really want to eat. Kids don't want to eat wholesome foods: kids want to eat grease and sugar. This is why, given the choice, kids will eat things that do not qualify as food at all, such as Cheez Doodles, Yoo-Hoo, Good & Plenty, and those little wax bottles that contain colored syrup with enough sugar per bottle to dissolve a bulldozer in two hours. As kids grow up, they reluctantly accept the idea that their diets should be balanced, and by the time they are thirty-five or forty years old they will eat peas voluntarily. But all of us, deep in our hearts, still want grease and sugar. That is what separates us from animals.

And that is why fast-food restaurants are so successful. At fast-food restaurants, you never run the risk of finding peas on your plate. You don't even get a plate. What you get is hamburgers and French fries; these are your primary sources of grease. You get your sugar from soft drinks or "shakes," which are milk shakes from which the milk has been eliminated on the grounds that milk has been identified by the United States Government as a major cause of nutrition.

At first, fast-food restaurants were popular only with wild teenaged hot rodders who carried switchblade knives and refused to eat Brussels sprouts. But then the fast-food chains realized they could make much more money if they could broaden their appeal, so they started running television ads to convince people, particularly mothers, that fast food is *wholesome*. You see these ads all the time: you have your wholesome Mom and your wholesome Dad and their 2.2 wholesome kids, and they're at the fast-food restaurant, just wolfing down grease and sugar, and they're having such a wholesome time that every now and then everybody in the whole place, including the counterpersons with the "Star Trek" uniforms, jumps up and sings and dances out of sheer joy. The message is clear: You can *forget* about the old Balanced Diet Theory; it's *okay* to eat this stuff.

Lately, the advertisements have started stressing how much *variety* you can get at fast-food restaurants. Besides hamburger, you can get chicken in a hamburger bun, roast beef in a hamburger bun, steak in a hamburger bun, and fish in a hamburger bun; you can even get an entire three-part breakfast in a hamburger bun. A fast-food restaurant near me recently started serving—I swear this is true—*veal parmigiana* in a hamburger bun. And people are *buying* it.

This leads me to my plan to make several million

dollars. My plan rests on two assumptions:

• People have become so committed to fast food that they don't care *what* they eat, as long as it's in a hamburger bun, and

• There must be an enormous world glut of green vegetables, since nobody believes in the Balanced Diet Theory anymore.

So I plan to buy several tons of Brussels sprouts, which I figure would cost a total of six dollars. I'll put them in hamburger buns, then get some actor to dress up as a clown or some other idiot character and go on television and urge everybody to rush right over and pay me $1.69 for a Sprout McBun. Before long, kids will be *begging* their parents to buy my Brussels sprouts, and I will be rich. I'll bet you wish you had thought of it.

Rooting for Rutabagas

WARNING: This column contains highly sensitive information about U.S. nuclear strategy and rutabagas.

From time to time, we newspaper columnists obtain classified government documents that we share with our readers so we can protect the Public's Right to Know and make large sums of money. A good example is the famous columnist Jack Anderson, who is always revealing government secrets:

WASHINGTON—Classified documents recently obtained by this reporter indicate that Interior Secretary James Watt is secretly drafting legislation to legalize the shooting of American Indians for sport.

Over the years, Jack has obtained classified documents proving that every elected official in the United States is a worthless piece of scum. He gets classified documents in the mail as often as normal people get *Reader's Digest* sweepstakes offers. It has gotten to the point where high government officials routinely call Jack for information:

PRESIDENT REAGAN: Hello, Jack?

JACK ANDERSON: Hi, Mr. President. What can I do for you today?

REAGAN: Jack, I can't remember the procedure I'm supposed to use if I want to put the armed forces on Red Alert.

ANDERSON: Let's see . . . here it is. You call 800-411-9789 toll-free, and you say: "Buford ate a fat newt."

REAGAN: "Buford ate a bat suit?"

ANDERSON: No, that one launches a nuclear attack. It's "fat newt."

REAGAN: "Cat shoot." Got it. Thanks a million, Jack.

ANDERSON: Any time.

I would love to share some classified documents with you, but nobody ever sends me any. Mostly what I get in the mail is threats to sue me or kill me, along with the occasional crank letter. I did, however, recently receive some information that, as far as I know, has not been revealed in any other column. It concerns a topic that few Americans know anything about, and government officials never discuss publicly: rutabagas.

This information came in the form of a press release

248

from the Ontario Rutabaga Producers' Marketing Board. Ontario is located in Canada, a foreign country. So what we have is a group of foreign persons who are trying to influence Americans to buy rutabagas, and possibly even eat them.

Rutabagas, which belong to the turnip family, are fat roots ("Buford ate a fat root") that grow underground in Canada, which is Mother Nature's way of telling us she does not want us to eat them. Rutabagas have never been really big in America. Most Americans can go for days at a time without even thinking about them. Unless you live in a community where recreational drug use is widespread, you almost never hear anybody say: "Gee, I'd love to accept those free tickets to the final game of the World Series, but I want to get right home for dinner. We're having rutabagas."

The Ontario rutabaga producers are trying to influence American opinion by planting pro-rutabaga statements in newspaper food sections. This is fairly easy to do, because food-section editors are desperate for new recipes. There are only about eight dishes that Americans will actually eat, and all the food sections have printed every possible variation of the recipes, so nowadays they'll print anything:

SPAM, WHEAT CHEX ADD ZEST TO SPICY GRAPEFRUIT STEW

So the food sections will be easy prey for the rutabaga producers. Fairly soon, you will begin seeing statements like these, taken from the press release: "Ontario rutabagas give you good taste and good food value in cold, wet winters . . . as a fresh snack or served in exciting gourmet dishes . . . covered in a thin wax

249

coating . . . use a good sharp knife to cut off the purple top . . ." Your children will read these statements, and then one cold, wet winter day they will come home, refuse the plate of good, traditionally American Twinkles you have thoughtfully prepared, and demand instead that you whack the purple tops off of wax-covered Canadian roots and serve them as snacks.

And as sure as night follows day, once we start eating rutabagas, there will be nothing to prevent us from going directly to leeks. I recently obtained an extremely pro-leek press release from an outfit that calls itself the United Fresh Fruit and Vegetable Association, which is headquartered in Alexandria, Virginia, but obviously takes its orders directly from a foreign government, because it openly uses words such as "vichyssoise." Here is a direct quotation, which I would refuse to print if the national interest were not at stake: "The Scottish use leeks in a traditional favorite, Cock-a-Leekie Soup, which has many delicious variations." If you start hearing talk like this from your children, don't say I didn't warn you.

I could go on—I could tell you about the California Dried Fig Advisory Board, which recently blanketed the nation with a document called the "Fig News"—but I don't have the space. I will do my best to keep you abreast of this important story until Jack Anderson picks it up, or I am found stabbed to death with a good, sharp, purple-stained knife.

Traveling Light

Vacation Reservations

THIS IS THE TIME of year to gather up your family and all your available money and decide what you're going to do on your summer vacation. You should get an opinion from everybody, including your children, because, after all, they are family members too, even though all they do is sit around and watch television and run up huge orthodontist bills and sneer at plain old affordable U.S. Keds sneakers, demanding instead elaborate designer athletic footwear that costs as much per pair as you paid for your first car. On second thought, the heck with what your children want to do. You can notify them of your vacation plans via memorandum.

The cheapest vacation is the kind where you just stay home, avoiding the hassle and expense of travel and getting to know each other better as a family and gagging with boredom. Another option is to put the whole family into the car and take a trip. That's what my family did, back in the fifties. We usually went to Florida, which has a lot of tourist attractions, always announced by large, fading roadside signs:

SEE THE WORLD'S OLDEST SHELL MUSEUM
AND SNAKE RODEO—1 MILE

We had a system for car travel. My father would drive; my mother would periodically offer to drive, knowing that my father would not let her drive unless he went blind in both eyes and lapsed into a coma; and my sister and I would sit in the backseat and read Archie

253

comic books for the first 11 miles, then punch each other and scream for the remaining 970. My father tended to stop at a lot of tourist attractions, so he could walk around and smoke cigarettes and try to persuade himself not to lock my sister and me in the trunk and abandon the car.

I bet we stopped at every tourist attraction in Florida. A lot of them involved alligators, which are as common in Florida as retirees. You'd pay your money and go into this fenced-in area that was rife with alligators, which sounds dangerous but wasn't, because alligators are the most jaded reptiles on earth. They'd just lie around in the muck with their eyes half-open, looking like they'd been out playing cards and drinking for four consecutive nights. Sometimes, to liven things up, a tourist-attraction personnel would wrestle an alligator. This was always advertised as a death-defying feat, but the alligators never seemed interested. They would just lie there, hung over, while the tourist-attraction personnel dragged them around for a few minutes. It was as exciting as watching somebody move a large carpet. I would have much preferred to watch two tourist-attraction personnel wrestle each other, and I imagine the alligators would have agreed.

These days, the tourist attractions in Florida are much more educational. For example, Disney World has rides where you get in these little cars and travel through a gigantic replica of a human heart, pausing in the aorta to see an electronic robot imitate Abraham Lincoln giving the Gettysburg Address, then zipping down a chute and splashing into a pond. Another educational thing to do on vacation is visit an authentic colonial historic site, where people in authentic colonial garb demonstrate how our ancestors made candles by hand. I'd say one historic site is plenty, because, let's face it, after you've watched people make candles for a few minutes, you're ready to go back to watching people haul alligators around.

Your biggest vacation expenses, besides tourist-attraction admission fees, are food and lodging. You can keep your food costs down by eating at one of the many fine roadside stands, such as the Dairy Queen, the Dairy Freeze, the Dairy King, the Frozen Dairy Queen, the Freezing King of the Dairy, the Dozing Fairy Queen, and so on. Although many nutrition-conscious parents worry that the food sold at these stands is nothing more than sugar, the truth is that it also contains more than the minimum daily adult requirement of gelatin, which builds the strong fingernails children need in the backseat on long car trips.

Lodging is a trickier problem. If you don't mind outdoor pit toilets, you can stay at public campsites. On the other hand, if you don't mind outdoor pit toilets, you need psychiatric help. You can also look for cheap motels, the ones that have rooms for six dollars a night, but generally these rooms have 1952 Philco televisions and large tropical insects. So your best bet is to stay with friends or relatives. If you have no friends or relatives where you plan to vacation, you can still get free lodging if you use this proven system: Make a list of ten random names and addresses, with yours at the top. Then obtain the telephone directory for the area you want to visit, pick a dozen names at random, and send each one a copy of your list and this letter:

Do not throw away this letter! This is a chain letter! It was started by nuns shortly after the Korean War, and it has NEVER BEEN BROKEN! To keep the chain

255

going, all you have to do is provide lodging for a week for the family at the top of the enclosed list! Within a year, you will receive 1,285,312 offers of free lodging, enough free lodging to last for the rest of your life! If you break the chain, you will die a horrible death!

That should get you all the lodging you need. Have a swell trip, and be sure to write.

Trip to Balmy California

IF YOU'RE LOOKING for ways to develop a serious drinking problem, I urge you to take a small child across the country in an airplane. My wife and I did this recently, in an effort to get to California. We had heard that California contains these large red trees. Our vacation objective was to go out, look at the trees, and return to Pennsylvania without being assaulted by mass murderers, who abound in California.

One problem was that we missed our plane because it took off an hour and a half before our tickets said it would. I'm still not sure why. It was just one of those mysterious things that happen all the time in the world of commercial aviation. Maybe the airlines have so many delayed flights that every now and then they let one take off early just to even things out. All I know is that it looked as if our vacation was over before it began, which was fine with me, because our two-year-old son, Robert, had already gone into Public Behavior Mode, which is a snotty behavior pattern that modern children get into because they know that modern parents aren't allowed to strike them in public for fear of being reported to the police as child abusers.

256

While Robert was running around the airport looking for electrical outlets to stick his fingers into, an airlines person arranged to put us on a plane bound for St. Louis. We were not really interested in going to St. Louis, because the principal tourist attraction there is an arch. I once paid money and waited on line to go up to the top of this arch, and when I finally got there, I realized that (a) St. Louis looks basically the same from the top of the arch as from on the ground, only flatter; and (b) I had no way of knowing whether the people who built this arch were serious, competent arch builders or merely close friends and relations of the mayor whose arch would collapse at any moment. So I got back down, and have felt no great need to go to St. Louis since. But the airlines person assured us that St. Louis is in the same general direction as California. I think he mainly wanted to get Robert out of the airport.

The flight to St. Louis was uneventful, except that Robert and several other children were much more disruptive than terrorist hijackers and a passenger at the back of the plane died in what I believe was an unrelated incident. Also, my wife was fairly nervous. She doesn't believe that planes can actually fly, on the grounds that they are enormous objects filled with people, suitcases, and airline food, which is a very heavy kind of food, the idea being that if the passengers are given food that takes a long time to chew, they won't get bored. Despite my wife's concerns, we made it to St. Louis, where the airlines personnel, in another commercial-aviation mystery, put us in the first-class section of a plane bound for California. First class is for people who have paid a lot of extra money so they won't have to sit in the same section as small children. Robert sensed this immediately and went into Extended Public Behavior Mode, a mode that baffles medical science because in it a child can cry for more than forty-five minutes *without inhaling.* Robert wanted the stewardess to open the airplane door, only we were 35,000 feet in the air. After a while, I got the impression the stewardess was seriously considering opening the door for him anyway.

Eventually we got to California and saw the trees. They were large and red, just as we had been told. I liked them better than the St. Louis arch, because you didn't have to go up in them. Robert liked them because they were surrounded by reddish, clingy dirt that you can get into your hair and diaper really easily.

We also drove down the Pacific coast on a winding road that offered many spectacular views that I couldn't look at for fear I would plunge the car into the ocean. Fortunately, my wife took many pictures, and I intend to look at them once we save up enough money to have them developed.

We planned to end our vacation in Los Angeles, but we never actually located it. We'd get on a large road and follow the signs that said "Los Angeles," but we'd always wind up in some place whose name ended in the letter *a*, such as Pomona and Ventura, filled with stores selling waterbeds. I'm sure Los Angeles was around there somewhere, because you'd need a city with a large population to support a waterbed industry that big.

We did find Disneyland. Disneyland is basically an enormous amusement park, except that, thanks to the vision and creative genius of the immortal Walt Disney, it has clean rest rooms. There are lots of simulated things to do in Disneyland. We went on a simulated paddle-wheel riverboat ride through a simulated wild frontier. On the simulated riverbanks, we saw a scene in which simulated evil Indians had shot a simulated arrow through the chest of a simulated white settler. Farther on, we saw some more simulated Indians; the riverboat announcer identified these as good Indians. I strongly suspect they had been installed after the evil Indians, when the Disneyland executives decided they ought to present a more balanced picture. We never saw any evil white settlers.

The most exciting part of Disneyland for Robert was when he met Mickey Mouse. Robert had seen mice, but they were small and naked, so when he was suddenly confronted with this mouse who was wearing a suit and whose head was the size of a refrigerator carton, he was very concerned. He still talks about it. "That big mouse," he says. He'll probably carry the memory for the rest of his life. Someday he may even sue.

Finally, it was time to leave sunny California, so we got on another plane that did not leave at the time shown on our tickets. But it also didn't stop in St. Louis, so we were pleased. We plan to go again sometime, when Robert has reached a more appropriate age, such as forty.

The Plane Truth

THERE ARE MANY things you can do during a long airplane flight to take your mind off the fact that you are several miles up in the air in a heavy object built and operated by people you don't even know, people who could well be insane careless suicidal drug addicts. For one thing, you can listen to the Safety Lecture given by the flight attendants (who were known as "stewardesses" before some of them became males) just before the plane takes off. The flight attendants demonstrate the safety features of the plane, the main one being little plastic bags that pop out of the ceiling when the plane starts to crash. You're supposed to put a bag over your mouth and breathe from it; this ensures that you will have an adequate supply of oxygen until the plane hits the ground at three or four hundred miles an hour. Another safety feature is that the seats float, so the airline can retrieve them if the plane crashes into the ocean.

When you get right down to it, the Safety Lecture is a silly idea. I mean, if the passengers really thought the plane was going to *crash*, they wouldn't get on it in the first place, let alone learn how to get an adequate oxygen supply on the way down. As a result, most passengers pay no attention whatsoever to the safety lecture. The flight attendants know this, and, out of sheer boredom, they long ago stopped reading the Official Safety Lecture Script. Next time you're on a plane, listen closely to what they actually say:

"Hi, I'm Debbie, the chief flight attendant, and on behalf of the entire crew I'd like to welcome you aboard Flight 302 to Bermuda. Much of our flight will be over water, so I'd like to remind you that if we do crash, there is an excellent chance that those of us who survive will be eaten by sharks. Please note that various windows are designated as emergency exits, the kind that have been known to pop open for no good reason at extremely high altitudes. Now if you will look at the front of the cabin, one of the flight attendants will demonstrate how to seal Tupperware containers. Thank you and we hope you enjoy the flight."

After the Safety Lecture comes the takeoff, which is terrifying until you realize that the pilot has probably taken off thousands of times without a mishap, which means that the odds of a mishap occurring get better every time. Once you're in the air, you get the Pilot's Message:

"Good afternoon, this is Pilot Horvel Grist speaking. My copilot and I are up here with a whole batch of dials and gauges and controls of every kind, but everything seems to be pretty much the way they described it in Pilot School. We'll be cruising along at an altitude of thirty-eight thousand feet, and we should reach our destination just about on schedule, after which we'll circle it for five or six hours. That large object we're passing over right now is Pittsburgh. Or the Grand Canyon. We'll let you know once we pin it down."

Sometimes the pilot lets you listen in on his conversations with Air Traffic Control. Pilots are always talking to Air Traffic Control to make sure they go in the right directions and don't whack into anything in midair. These conversations are conducted in crisp, professional language:

PILOT: Come in, Air Traffic Control. This is a great big jet up in the sky.

AIR TRAFFIC CONTROLLER: A great big *what?*

PILOT: Jet.

AIR TRAFFIC CONTROLLER: Oh, *jet.* I thought you said *pet.* I was picturing this huge Russian wolfhound whizzing around up there.

PILOT *(panicking):* Did you say there's a huge Russian missile in the air?

AIR TRAFFIC CONTROLLER *(screaming):* My

261

God! There's a huge Russian missile in the air! Somebody notify the Strategic Air Command!

PILOT: I'm going to try to land on the Interstate.

Another fun thing to do during long plane trips is read the paperback books they sell in airports. There are three kinds:

• Spy thrillers, in which evil people, usually Nazis left over from World War II, nearly blow up the world or kill the President or the Pope. If airport books are any indication, there are at least 450,000 evil Nazi World War II geniuses still at large, many of them with atomic laser cannons. Look for a large swastika on the cover; this is the publishing industry's way of letting you know it's a fun book.

• Supernatural thrillers, in which the devil possesses people. Possession by the devil used to be fairly rare—I remember when it was just that little girl in *The Exorcist*—but these days it's as common as strep throat. Before long, we'll have special schools for possessed people, and the government will start requiring large corporations to hire them.

• Dirty books, in which you can turn to any page at random and start reading, because you already know what's going to happen, so the only question is how many times. Dirty-book characters live lives that differ substantially from yours and mine. For example, if *you* walk into a restaurant, you will sit down, order dinner, eat, pay, and leave. Here's what happens to a dirty-book character in a restaurant:

John glanced up from the menu and suddenly realized, as six statuesque waitresses and two slim Siamese busboys sidled up to him, that he was the lone customer in the restaurant. "We have a special tonight," said one of the waitresses, gesturing toward the steam table.

The only other way to pass the time on long plane flights is to get hijacked by armed fanatic terrorists. If you have no armed fanatic terrorists on your flight, you can liven things up yourself by making clever hijacking jokes. For example, when the flight attendants serve dinner, you can stand up and wave your chicken pie aloft, announcing in a loud voice that it is actually an explosive device that you plan to detonate unless the plane goes to Zaire. The airplane crew will find this a very amusing diversion from the boring routine, and will give you lots of extra attention. Another benefit is that you won't have to eat the chicken pie, which probably tastes like an explosive device anyway.

Destination: Maybe

I FLY A LOT, because of the nature of my job. I'm a gnat.

Ha ha. Just a little humor there to introduce today's topic, which is air travel. As a businessperson, I have to travel by air a lot because modern corporations have many far-flung plants. The plants are flung as far as possible so modern corporation presidents will have an excuse to fly around the country in corporate jets drinking martinis at 550 miles an hour. The rest of us have to fly via commercial airliner, which is less pleasant because federal law requires commercial airliners to carry infants trained to squall at altitudes above two hundred feet. This keeps the passengers calm, because they're all thinking, "I wish somebody

263

would stuff a towel into that infant's mouth," which prevents them from thinking, "I am thirty-five thousand feet up in the air riding in an extremely sophisticated and complex piece of machinery controlled by a person with a Southern accent."

Actually, there's nothing to worry about, except the possibility that all the engines will fail at once and the plane will drop like a rock. And even if this happens, airplanes have all kinds of backup safety devices, by which I mean little, masks that pop out of the ceiling. You're supposed to put one of these over your mouth so the pilot won't hear you screaming while he radios for instructions on how to get the engines started again, assuming the radio still works. So you're actually much safer flying in an airplane than riding in a car, although needless to say this ceases to be true once the airplane hits the ground. But as long as the plane is in the air and the engines are going, the only bad thing that can happen is that it will fly into another plane, which is why we have air traffic controllers.

In the old days, air traffic controllers sat and stared at little radar screens so long that they eventually went crazy, so Ronald Reagan, who is firmly opposed to having crazy federal employees below the Cabinet level, fired them all and got a new batch. Needless to say the new controllers don't want to make the same mistake as their predecessors, so they've learned how to relax on the job. Their motto is "Tomorrow's another day," and their approach is low-key:

PILOT: This is Flight 274, requesting landing instructions.

CONTROLLER: Well, if it was *me,* I would put the wheels down first, but don't quote me on that.

PILOT: No, I already know how to *land* I was hoping you could tell me which runway I should land on.

CONTROLLER: Ah. Let me just turn on the little screen here, and—There we are. Say, is that you about to plow into the mountain?

PILOT: No.

CONTROLLER: Oh. That must be one of Bob's. *(Yelling to another controller.)* Bob, could you turn your screen on for a second? One of your planes is about to—Wait, forget it.

PILOT: Um, look, we're running out of fuel here, so I'd really appreciate it if you could possibly—

CONTROLLER: Hey, lighten up, will you? Do you want to make me tense and crazy so Reagan can fire me? *(Yelling to the other controllers)* Hey, guys! I think I got a Republican here! *(Laughter in background, shouts of "Steer him into the mountain!")*

PILOT: Look please—

CONTROLLER: Hey, no sweat. We're just having some fun. I'll get back to you with a runway right after my break.

PILOT: But—

CONTROLLER: *(Click.)*

HERE ARE SOME TIPS for making your trip more enjoyable:

• *Never believe anything airline employees say about when a plane will land or take off.* No matter how badly the schedule is screwed up, they will claim everything is fine, because otherwise you might realize it would be faster to walk to your destination. Let's say

265

you're waiting for Flight 206, which is an hour late, and you ask an agent at the ticket counter when it's due in. He'll punch a few buttons on his computer, which will give him this message: "FLIGHT 206 HAS CRASH-LANDED ON A REMOTE CORAL REEF IN THE SOUTH PACIFIC AND ALL THE TIRES ARE FLAT AND THE ENGINES ARE BROKEN AND THE PASSENGERS AND CREW ARE BEING HELD AT GUNPOINT BY HIJACKERS ARMED WITH NUCLEAR WEAPONS AND THERE IS A VERY HEAVY FOG." The agent will look you cheerfully in the eye and say: "It should be here any minute now."

• *Never let anybody take your luggage.* Airline employees will continually try to snatch it from you; you must ward them off with a stiff forearm and flee on foot. If they corner you, toss your luggage out the window, or set it on fire—anything to prevent it from falling into their hands, because God alone knows what will happen to it then.

• *Never pull out a machine gun and fire thirty thousand rounds into those leechlike religious cult members who approach you in airports and try to get you to give them money.* Some stray bullets could conceivably hit innocent bystanders, and then you would feel terrible.

The Sporting Life

Unsportsmanlike Conduct

I FIRST GOT involved in organized sports in fifth grade, when, because of federal law, I had to join the Little League. In Little League we played a game that is something like baseball, except in baseball you are supposed to catch, throw, and hit a ball, whereas most of us Little Leaguers could do none of these things.

Oh, there were a few exceptions, fast-developing boys with huge quantities of adolescent hormones raging through their bodies, causing them to have rudimentary mustaches and giving them the ability to throw a ball at upwards of six hundred miles an hour, but with no idea whatsoever where it would go. These boys always got to pitch, which presented a real problem for the rest of us, because in Little League the pitcher stands eight feet from home plate. The catcher got to wear many protective garments, and the umpire got to wear protective garments *and* hide behind the catcher. But all we batters got to wear was plastic helmets that fell off if we moved our heads.

I hated to bat. I used to pray that the kids ahead of me would strike out, or that I would get appendicitis, or that a volcano would erupt in center field before my turn came. I was very close to God when I was in Little League. But sometimes He would let me down, and I'd have to bat. In the background, the coach would yell idiot advice, such as "Keep your eye on the ball." This was easy for *him* to say: *he* always stood over by the bench, well out of harm's way.

I made no effort to keep my eye on the ball. I concentrated exclusively on avoiding death. I would

269

stand there, trying to hold my head perfectly still so my helmet wouldn't fall off, and when the prematurely large kid who was pitching let go of the ball, I would swing the bat violently, in hopes of striking out or deflecting the ball before it could smash into my body. Usually I struck out, which was good, because then I could go back to the safety of the bench and help the coach encourage some other terrified kid to keep his eye on the ball. I much preferred to play in the field, especially the outfield. If a batter got a hit, you could run like a maniac, and the odds were that you'd be several hundred feet away from the ball by the time it landed.

I understand that Little League was supposed to teach me the rules of sportsmanship. The main rule of sportsmanship I learned was: Never participate in a sport where the coach urges you to do insane and dangerous things that he himself does not do. Football is another good example. If you watch a football game, you'll notice that the coaches constantly urge the players to run into each other at high speeds, but the coaches themselves tend to remain on the sidelines.

So after I fulfilled my legal commitment to Little League, I avoided organized sports and got my exercise in the form of minor vandalism. But when I got to high school, I discovered that I had to go out for an organized sport so I could be called up to the auditorium stage during the annual athletic awards assembly to receive a varsity letter.

I cannot overemphasize the importance the kids in my high school attached to varsity letters. You could be a bozo of astonishing magnitude, but if you had a varsity letter, you were bound to succeed socially. Oh, the school administrators tried to make academic achievements seem important, too. They'd have academic assemblies, where they'd call all the studious kids up onto the stage. But the rest of the kids were unimpressed. They'd sit there, wearing their varsity sweaters, and hoot and snicker while some poor kid with a slide rule dangling from his belt got the Math Achievement Award. No, to make it in my high school you had to have a varsity letter, which meant you had to go out for a sport.

So in my sophomore year I went out for track, because track was the sport where you were least likely to have something thrown at you or have somebody run into you at high speed. The event I chose was the long jump, because all you had to do was run maybe fifty feet, after which you leaped into a soft pit. That was it. The long jump was far superior to the other events, in which you were required to run as much as a mile without stopping.

Anyway, I spent a happy spring, leaping into the pit and dreaming about going up on the stage to get my varsity letter. Then one day we all piled into buses and rode, laughing and gesturing at motorists, to a rival school for a track meet. This proved to be my downfall, because it turned out that at track meets they measured how far we long jumpers jumped, and only the three longest jumpers got points, which you needed to get your varsity letter. I was not one of the three longest jumpers. I was not one of the ten longest jumpers. In fact, they could have pulled people out of the crowd, old people with arthritis, and *they* probably would have jumped farther than I did.

So that was the end of my involvement with organized sports. Fortunately, there was one other avenue to popularity in my high school, which was to drink several quarts of beer, go to a dance, and behave in such an extremely antisocial manner that you got thrown out by the assistant principal in full view of hundreds of admiring kids. So in the end I achieved social acceptance.

After I got out of high school, varsity letters seemed less important, and academic achievement started to seem more important. I mean, if you go to a cocktail party and subtly contrive to flash your varsity letter, people will think you are a jerk; whereas if you subtly contrive to flash your Phi Beta Kappa key, people will still think you are a jerk, but an educated jerk.

I often wonder what my former classmates do with their varsity letters, now that they're out of high school. Maybe they wear them in the privacy of their homes. Why not? I still drink beer.

Football Deflated

ONCE AGAIN it is time for Americans of all races and religions to set aside their petty differences and spend half a day drinking beer and watching large persons injure each other's knees. You guessed it: it's Super Bowl time.

The Super Bowl is an American tradition, like heart disease. You need not know anything about football to enjoy it. I know very little about football, and I intend to write a whole column about it and get paid for it.

First, let's talk about the word *football*. In most nations, when people say "football" they mean "soccer," which is a completely different game in which smallish persons whiz about on a field while the spectators beat each other up and eventually overthrow the government. I don't know why the other nations call soccer "football," but I suspect it has something to do with the metric system and I say the hell with it.

Modern American football was invented by college students. This should surprise nobody. There are no depths of idiocy to which college students will not sink. You're always reading about them in the newspapers:

FORT STUCCO, TEXAS—Six members of Beta Beta Zoot Fraternity here at Dunderson State Agricultural, Astronomical, and Aeronautical Technical College are attempting to raise money for charity and get their names in the Guinness Book of World Records *by setting a record for squatting around in the dirt drinking beer. They have been at it for eight days now, or possibly longer; a spokesbrother for the group said the Beta Betas spend a fair amount of time squatting in the dirt drinking beer anyway, so nobody knows for sure when they started doing it for charity. "We just thought, you know, we'd do something, you know, to make the world a better place and whatnot," he said. "We're gonna give the money to charity if we get any money and can find a charity or something to give the money to, if we get any money". The spokesbrother said the rest of the student body has supported the effort by not driving cars over any of the brothers.*

Anyway, the first modern intercollegiate American football game was played in 1869 between Rutgers and Princeton, two schools which are located in New Jersey, which should also surprise nobody. Rutgers won that game, and Princeton won the rematch a week later, but both schools were barred from postseason bowl competition because of recruiting violations.

Over the next hundred years or so football saw a great many major innovations and refinements that are too boring to even think about. Along the way professional football came into being so the largest and most violent college players would have a way to earn money other than simply demanding it from innocent civilians.

Today the National Football League has several dozen teams, which play games starting in about August and running right through to January. This presents many scheduling problems, because some of the teams are in warm places where everybody wants to play, and some are in cold places where nobody wants to play. Along about December you'll have four or five teams showing up to play the Miami Dolphins and none showing up to play the Minnesota Vikings. So what happens is the Dolphins end up fielding eleven men who get the stuffing knocked out of them by fifty-five opponents, while the Vikings win by scores of 12,324 to nothing. This is called the "home field advantage."

At the end of the season, the teams with the fewest major injuries meet in the Super Bowl. By this time, of course, the players can barely walk, let alone run around and knock each other down, so the Super Bowl is usually pretty awful. To get people to watch, league officials try to turn it into a Major Spectacle, along the lines of the fall of the Roman Empire. I remember one year, during the Nixon administration, when they had Air Force jet fighters fly over the stadium during the national anthem. I believe that was also the year that George Allen, one of the coaches, actually had his players run a play suggested by Nixon. In Nixon's

274

play, the quarterback gets the ball, then, when the other team's linemen are about to jump on him, claims that he doesn't have the ball, in fact has *never* had the ball, and implies that several of his teammates may have the ball, but because of National Security they can't talk about it.

But back to the jets. The trouble with having jets fly over the stadium during the national anthem is that next year people expect something even *more* spectacular, like having the jets shoot down the Goodyear Blimp. I am not *endorsing* this idea, you understand. I'm just explaining football.

Gunning for Safety

YOU NEED A WAY to defend yourself, because there is a lot of violence these days. For example, recently a motorist drove into one of the bushes on my property in a violent manner. If I had had a gun, I could have gone out and defended the bush, but as it was I had to stand there helplessly, unarmed, while the motorist offered to replace it. I turned down the offer because I hate my bushes, which spend their days lunging out and scratching at me when I mow the lawn. I periodically go out with my chain saw and prune them down to the size of poinsettias, but that just angers them, and within days they are back, bigger and more hostile than before. To be honest, I wouldn't be bothered in the least if motorists lobbed grenades at them as they drove by. But that is not the point. The point is that we all need some way to defend ourselves.

The main reason violence is increasing, of course, is television. At one time, all the violence was on television and the streets were safe, because everybody was home watching it. You had shows like "Starsky and Hutch," where you didn't dare go to the bathroom for fear you would miss some violence. Starsky and Hutch were police officers who believed that the only way to stop a crime—robbery, jaywalking, tax evasion—was to drive their car very fast through a populated area while shooting their guns out the window. They were very effective, largely because people refused to go out on the street for fear of being run over and shot.

But these days they're not allowed to show violence on television except on Saturday-morning cartoon shows for children aged five and under. The rest of us are stuck with shows like "Donahue" and "Dallas," in which people drone on endlessly about sex but never actually do anything on the screen. After watching these shows for a few hours, viewers tend to get bored and go out on the street and commit acts of violence.

Another reason violence is increasing is electronic arcade games. Arcade games cause violence because they encourage teenagers to shoot at alien beings who are trying to destroy the Earth. The teenagers are getting very good at this. A skilled teenager can defend the entire planet for a quarter; in contrast, the United States government spends roughly $100 billion just to defend the Western Europeans, all of whom hate us. The problem is that the government can get all the dollars it wants merely by threatening to throw taxpayers in jail, whereas the teenagers must get their quarters by badgering their parents. Eventually the parents get irritated, especially if they have been watching television, and this leads to violence.

How can you defend yourself? One excellent method is to get a vicious dog. You don't want a large dog, such as a German shepherd, because large dogs are so accustomed to getting respect that they have completely forgotten how to attack. They rely entirely on deep growls and snarls, which are useless against an intruder wearing earplugs or a Sony Walkman. So what you want to get is a small, insecure dog, such as a miniature French poodle, which knows how stupid it looks and consequently hates everybody. If you want it to be really vicious, you should give it a silly haircut and make it wear a fake-jewel collar and sit in your lap. After a few days of this, it will attack anything that moves, including you, but this is a small price to pay for peace of mind.

You can also defend yourself with guns. The U.S. Constitution says that the government cannot stop you from owning a gun. The courts have interpreted this to mean that the government can stop you from owning a gun, so you'd better check your local laws before you buy one. If you do get a gun, you should join your local Gun Fondlers Club and learn the Rules of Gun Safety, which are:

1. Never load your gun.
2. Never clean your gun.
3. Never even take your gun out of the box.
4. Never point your gun at anything or anybody except your vicious little dog if it really gets out of line.

If you don't want to own a gun, you can take up karate, a form of martial arts in which people who have had years and years of training can, using only their hands and feet, make some of the worst movies in the history of the world. They can also break boards, which could be very useful if an intruder enters your home and tries to hide behind your spare lumber so the dog can't get at him. I like the idea of learning to break boards with my bare hands. It's a skill I might be able to use on my bushes.

Something Fishy Here

FISHING IS AN excellent way to relax and contemplate the beauty of nature and get in touch with your inner self and maim and kill fish. Many people would be much happier if they went fishing. Take Secretary of State Alexander Haig. He seems *awfully* tense. I think he should take four or eight years off, buy several hundred six-packs, and go fishing. Al would probably shoot the fish with a bazooka, but what the heck, as long as he doesn't start a nuclear war or something.

It's okay to kill fish. It's not like hunting, where you kill friendly brown-eyed woodland creatures like Bambi and Thumper who talk in squeaky little voices. Fish are bad. They go to the bathroom in public waters, and they eat teenagers, as was demonstrated in the fine nature movies *Jaws* and *Jaws 2*. Besides, fish can't feel anything. I know this because I took a fish apart once, in biology class. The idea was that I would find a little fish heart and a little fish stomach and a little fish nervous system, like the diagram in the biology textbook. I found none of these things. All I found was glop. Fish are nothing but little bags of glop swimming around with fish heads in front, so don't waste your pity.

IMPORTANT NOTE: When I talk about fish, I am not talking about whales. Whales are mammals: they have feelings and can talk to each other, just like you and me. The only difference between whales and humans is that whales mate for life. Some evil foreign persons, such as the Japanese and the Russians, kill whales. The Japanese use them to make efficient automobiles, which they force Americans to buy so American auto workers will lose their jobs. The Russians don't do anything with their whales. They just use whaling as an excuse to get away from Russia for a couple of months.

IF YOU WANT TO FISH, you have to decide whether to catch freshwater fish or saltwater fish. The main saltwater fish are tuna, swordfish, catamaran, eel, oyster, snook, snipe, wahoo, giant clam, and serpent. To catch them, you have to go to the Bermuda Triangle in a small boat for several days. If you need more information on this subject, read *The Old Man and the Sea,* a book by Ernest Hemingway, a famous dead writer. In the book, the old man battles a huge fish for a long time, after which the fish tips the boat over and kills everybody except Ishmael. No, wait, that's *Moby-Dick.* Anyway, if you catch a big fish, the government requires you to have your picture taken with the fish hanging next to you in case it was stolen. Then you can take it home and either stuff it and hang it on your wall or, if you have any taste at all, just throw it in the garbage.

The main freshwater fish are bass, bream, guppy, carp, frog, muskellunge, piccolo, and crappie. Some people claim there are also trout, but this is a mythical fish, like the Loch Ness Monster. Nobody in recorded history has ever even *seen* a trout, let alone caught one. I went "trout fishing" once, with my friend Neil and his uncle Bruce. We'd wander around these streams, and every now and then Uncle Bruce would point to a shallow pool of water that any fool could see contained

279

absolutely no fish. "That's where the trout will be," he'd say, and Neil and I would stand there and not catch fish for several hours while Uncle Bruce went back to the tent to drink. I believe his marriage was in trouble.

Some people still believe in trout. You'll see them out by streams on the first day of trout season, standing shoulder to shoulder. The humorous thing is that they think the way to catch these mythical trout is to wave long strings with fuzzy hooks around in the air. I mean, they hardly ever even put them in the *water,* for heaven's sake. If there were such a thing as a trout, the only way it would get caught is if it leaped out of the water and grabbed a hook as it flew by.

If you want to fish for fish that actually exist, you'll need either bait or lures. The best bait is worms, which you can find almost anywhere worms are found. All you do is impale the worm on the hook, wait for the little worm screams to die down, and toss it in the water. The fish will come around and nibble on it until it's gone, then they'll give the hook a gentle tug to let you know it's time to send another worm down.

You can also use artificial lures, which are brightly colored plastic or metal things with hooks on them that are scientifically designed so they appear to fish to be brightly colored plastic or metal things with hooks on them. Fish *love* lures. They gather together in little lure-appreciation groups, called "schools," and howl with laughter as the lures go by. It's their major form of entertainment, and they don't want to lose it, so every now and then they draw lots and the loser has to bite the lure and get caught. This encourages the fishermen to continue.

Tips from the Bottom

Serf Wanted

I THINK EVERYBODY should have a career. Careers give you money and a place to go during weekdays when there's nothing good on television.

No doubt many of you young people out there would like to have careers, but can't find good jobs to start your careers with. Believe me, things are much better now than they used to be. In the Middle Ages, for example, the only good jobs were king and nobleman, and there were very few openings. So most people had to settle for serf or barbarian. The "Help Wanted" sections in the Middle Ages newspapers looked like this:

SERF WANTED—Must have experience sleeping with goats and whacking at soil with stick. Must have own stick. Goats provided.

BARBARIANS WANTED—Looting, some pillaging. Must get along well with other members of horde. Apply at tent of Howard the Unusually Large.

These jobs offered little opportunity to advance. If you were really good at serf, you might work yourself up to peasant, but that was about it. If you were really good at barbarian, after twenty years the head barbarian would give you a gold watch, then kill you and take it back.

Things are much better today. But you young folks still must be careful about how you prepare for your careers, because otherwise you may be misled. For example, you have probably seen those television ads claiming that if you join the armed forces, you'll get all kinds of useful career skills. You know the ads I mean:

they show people repairing tanks and jumping out of airplanes at six o'clock in the morning. Now I'm not saying these are not useful skills: I'm just saying that executives at major corporations, such as IBM, rarely repair tanks, and virtually never jump out of airplanes. Successful executives usually wait until their airplanes have landed.

Another source of bad career advice is school. Your teachers will tell you that the way to get a good job is to memorize such things as the capital of Bolivia. Do you think that your average successful corporate executive can name the capital of Bolivia? Don't be silly. I'll tell you who can name the capital of Bolivia: your teacher, that's who. Do you want to be a teacher? Do you want to spend your days trying to convince a bunch of snotty kids that they should memorize the capital of Bolivia? Of course not. You want to make large sums of money and have a nice office with various buttons you can push when you want coffee. So what you want to do is memorize as little useless information as you can in school. And as soon as you graduate, you should apply for a job in the government.

The government is loaded with terrific jobs. For example, you might want to be an ex-president. Here's a lifetime job, with excellent pay and benefits, that virtually any incompetent can do. The only real duty ex-presidents have is to write their memoirs, which nobody ever reads anyway. If you were an ex-president, you could turn in Volume Four of the *Encyclopaedia Britannica* (Ceylon—Congreve) and claim it was your memoirs, and nobody would know the difference.

You could also apply for a job as Supreme Court Justice. The pay is excellent, and you cannot be fired unless you appear on national television naked or something. You don't even have to know anything about the law. If the Chief Justice asked you what you thought about a particular case, you'd answer: "Oh, I don't know, I can see both sides. What do you other justices think?" Then you'd vote with the majority. Your only other duty would be to wear a robe.

If you can't get a good government job, you may have to work for private industry, which is not as good, because many private employers expect you to work. The best job, of course, is corporation president, but even this has its pitfalls. For example, when Lee Iacocca was named president of Chrysler, he probably thought he would be able to spend his days sitting in his office, wearing expensive suits and signing the occasional document. Instead, he is regularly forced to appear in humiliating television commercials, in which he offers to *pay people money* if they will buy his cars.

I think the best private-industry job is construction worker. You may think this would be a difficult job, involving lifting heavy objects and assembling buildings. But if you look closely at a construction site, you'll notice the workers walk around a lot, drink coffee, and yell to each other, but, because of various clauses in their contracts, *they never actually build anything.* I'm not sure who really builds buildings; I suspect it's done at night, perhaps by serfs.

Wedding Etiquette

THIS IS AN excellent time of year to get married,what with the warm weather and all. As you may recall, it was around this time of year that Prince Charles and

Princess Diana got married in a ceremony that lasted, by my calculations, about two weeks. It took Charles nearly a half hour just to say "I do":

"I, Charles Arthur Philip George Henry Maurice Billy Bob Norman Howard Elmer the Third, Duke of the Realm, Defender of the Throne, Earl of Pillsbury, Lord of the Manse, Prince of a Fellow, Knight of the Trouser, Top of the Morning, Vice President of Marketing, and much, much more, do."

If you want to have a nice wedding, a really Special Day, you have to plan very carefully and follow the rules of wedding etiquette. Here's what you do:

GETTING ENGAGED

You should get engaged to somebody who has a job and will show up at the wedding. If you think your fiancé is unreliable, get engaged to several people, because there is no breach of etiquette worse than making your friends and relatives give you wedding presents and then failing to go through with it. If you get engaged to several people and they all show up, take all but one aside, tell them you won't be needing them, and give them each an inexpensive fondue set (you'll receive dozens as wedding gifts).

ANNOUNCING THE ENGAGEMENT

If you are a member of the working classes and have a name like Helvina Spackle, the newspapers won't print your engagement announcement, and you'll have to settle for a three-by-five card on the bulletin board at the supermarket. So if you want to make the social pages, your best bet is to use a name like Allison Weatherington-Huffington DuBois and send in a picture of Julie Andrews.

CHOOSING A CHURCH

You must do this carefully, because some churches won't let you get married in them unless you hold certain specific religious beliefs. Check this out in advance by calling the clergyman:

YOU: Hello. Could you tell me if you require people to have any specific religious beliefs?

CLERGYMAN: Why yes, we do.

YOU: How many?

CLERGYMAN: Let's see . . . five, six, seven . . . nine in all.

YOU: Fine. Can you send me a set?

THE INVITATION

Your invitation should consist of a large envelope containing several smaller envelopes in random sizes, a piece of tissue paper, and a card with these words:

Mr. and Mrs. Earl G. Spackle
Request the Honour and Favour
Of Your Attendance at the Marriage
Of Their Daughtour
Helvina Mae
(who is not pregnant)
To Elrood P. Budgewood
At the Manor Downs Vista Country Club
And Racquetball Court
Friday at around 4:30
RSVP   No Tank Tops

WHAT THE WEDDING PARTY SHOULD WEAR

The groom's party should wear pastel senior-prom-style outfits rented at the shopping mall. The bride's party should wear expensive dresses so unattractive that they can never be used again, even as tourniquets.

THE ORDER OF THE WEDDING PROCESSION
The first person down the aisle should be an adorable child belonging to the sister of the bride. If the bride's sister has no adorable child, she should rent one. Next comes the sister of the groom escorted by the maid of honor's boyfriend, followed by the niece of the maid of honor's boyfriend escorted by the oldest brother of the mother of the bride, followed by the oldest unmarried bridesmaid escorted by the youngest male member of the groom's family who has completed at least two years of college or technical school, followed by the great-grandmother of the bride (unless she is dead) escorted by the best man, followed, in order, by anyone else at the back of the church who is wearing nice clothes.

WHO PAYS FOR THE WEDDING
The family of the bride pays for the church, the clergyman, the limousines, the bridal gown, the flowers, the reception room, the band, the photographer, the hors d'oeuvre, the dinner, the cake, the liquor, and the honeymoon. The family of the groom eats a lot and gets tanked.

So there you have them, the rules of wedding etiquette. In a future column, I'll discuss the other two major etiquette areas, which are eating and death.

"Look! I Got You a Gift!"

WELL, the holiday gift-giving season is upon us once again, like an outbreak of shingles. Already I have received dozens of colorful mail-order gift catalogs urging me to buy bizarre objects and give them to people. I recently got a catalog featuring enormous cans of popcorn smeared with caramel, each containing enough carbohydrates to meet the needs of a medium-size industrial city for a year. If you want to give this gift, you just call the catalog people on their toll-free number and they ship a can to the person of your choice. It never even has to enter your home.

The question, of course, is, Why would you give such a gift? Do you know of anybody in the entire United States who would actually *want* a huge congealed mass of caramel popcorn? Of course not. This is an example of a holiday gift, which is an object whose primary purpose is to be given, not to actually be used. It expresses the ultimate holiday gift-giving message, which is, "Look! I got you a gift!" Another example is electric razors. Every year at this time, you see television commercials wherein a cartoon version of an electric razor shaves a cartoon face just as well as a cartoon razor blade, and thousands of women go out and buy $39.95 electric razors and give them to men ("Look! I got you a gift!"). And the men say, "Great! An electric razor!" Then they continue to use their nineteen-cent blade razors. They stick the electric razors into closets with their caramel-covered popcorn.

Men do the same thing to women. Every year I go to the department-store cosmetics counter, which emits a powerful aroma, reminiscent of a house of ill repute, and buy my wife one of the thirty thousand gift packages containing little designer tubes and jars with names like "Essence of Fragrance Moisturizing Body Cream," "Body of Essence Cream Moisturizing Fragrance," "Moist Fragrant Body Essential Creamer," et cetera. I don't know what these terms mean, and I don't care. All I know is I can say, "Look! I got you a gift!" I doubt my wife uses these things, because she lets my two-year-old son play with them, which means he routinely smells like a house of ill repute, but that's better than some of the things he smells like, if you get my drift.

But these are not the ultimate Holiday Gifts, because technically you could actually use them. I mean, you could use caramel-covered popcorn as attic insulation, and you could use an electric razor to crush insects. But many of the gifts that spring up in the holiday season reach a new level, the level of "pure holiday gift," which means you can't use them for anything except possibly ballast. For example:

• *Cute ceramic knick-knack figurines depicting animals, especially cats*—The way I see it, everybody who wants a cute ceramic cat has already bought one. It is cruel to inflict such objects on other people. I once was present when a holiday guest gave the hostess a ceramic cat, and she stood there, handling it as you would a live grenade, and trying desperately to think of an excuse not to put it on her mantel, which is the only thing you can do with a knick-knack. Eventually, of course, she had to put it on the mantel, and the entire room suddenly acquired an air of cuteness that no amount of expert interior decoration can disguise.

• *Guest soap formed into little balls or fruit shapes*—Nobody uses this soap. The people who live in the house don't use it, because it's for guests. The guests are afraid to use it, because they don't want to mess it up. They end up not washing their hands, which leads to the spread of infections. The government should put a stop to this soon, because it is only a matter of time before somebody starts selling guest soap shaped like cats.

• *Fruitcakes manufactured last April and packaged in cans and allowed to sit in a warehouse until they reach the density of a bowling ball*—These present all the problems of caramel-covered popcorn, with the added problem that they can cause hernias.

• *Coffee-table books*—These are gigantic books with lots of pictures and titles like *Scissors through the Ages* that you couldn't read even if you wanted to because the pages are all welded together from when your guests spilled banana daiquiris on them.

What can you do about this? You can buy gifts that people actually use. Think how happy you'd be if you got, say, a case of paper towels. Wouldn't that be terrific? That's what I'm going to get my wife this year. I'll bet she'll be speechless.

About Lawn Order

I GOT TO THINKING about ecology the other day when I ran over a turtle with my lawn mower. Now before you reptile lovers start sending me irate letters full of misspelled words, let me assure you that I was not

291

aiming for the turtle. I have enough trouble keeping my lawn mower in operation, and the last thing I would do is risk damaging it with a turtle. Let me also assure you that the turtle was unharmed, except for a few nicks on its shell that might make it less attractive to turtles of the opposite sex, whichever sex that happens to be. I don't know how you determine the sex of a turtle, and I don't want to know. I have come to think of this particular turtle as male, because my two-year-old son, who receives signals directly from outer space, recently announced that its name is Bob.

Bob has been hanging around our lawn for several months now, despite our efforts to encourage him to go into the woods with the other turtles. "These are the best years of your life, Bob," we say. "Don't waste them on our lawn." But Bob turns a deaf ear to our suggestions, assuming turtles have ears. You would think the lawn mower incident would have made him have second thoughts about our lawn, but lately he seems more attached to it than ever. This makes me think that maybe the theory of evolution is wrong after all. I figure that if turtles really had been evolving for all these years, they would have come up with something more intelligent than Bob.

Anyway, all this got me to thinking about ecology. Most wild animals are, like Bob, fairly stupid. Plants are even worse. It is up to us human beings to use our superior brains to protect them, or one day we will wake up to find there is no more nature, and we will no longer have any place to hold 1960s-style outdoor weddings.

So I am all for preserving wildlife, but I also think we have to use some judgment about it. We can't go around preserving *all* wildlife, because some of it is disgusting. Take insects, for example. The other night, while we were having dinner, some wildlife entered our house in the form of a flying insect that looked like a mosquito, but was large enough to play in the National Football League. It was the kind of insect that wouldn't even have to sting you, because it could crush you to death merely by landing on you.

Now I imagine that the president of the Sierra Club, sitting in the safety of his insect-free office, would say that we should have let this insect drone around the dining room until it broke a window and flew outside, where it would be eaten by another species, which would in turn be eaten by another species, and so on and so on, leading up the Great Chain of Life, until finally the second-to-last link in the chain is eaten by a nuclear physicist. But that is mere theory. The truth is that nothing around my house would have dared to eat this insect; in fact, it probably would have eaten Bob, shell and all. I bet that if the president of the Sierra Club had been in my house, he would have done exactly what I did, which was to leap up from the table and batter the insect repeatedly with a rolled-up newspaper.

So I propose that we direct our ecology efforts toward preserving those forms of wildlife that are safe and non-disgusting, namely:

• Cute, furry animals, such as seals and otters, that you see in Walt Disney nature movies, but never around your house.

• Large animals, such as elephants and boa constrictors, that live on other continents.

• Plants that produce flowers or eat insects.

• Turtles.

I have already embarked on a personal ecology effort to

293

preserve Bob. I have resolved that, despite the great personal sacrifice involved, I will no longer mow my lawn.

The Law vs. Justice

MOST OF US LEARN how the United States legal system works by watching television. We learn that if we obey the law, we will wind up chatting and laughing with attractive members of the opposite sex when the program ends, whereas if we break the law, we will fall from a great height onto rotating helicopter blades.

Some television shows explain the legal system in greater detail: they show actual dramatizations of court trials. The best such show was "Perry Mason," which starred Raymond Burr as a handsome defense attorney who eventually gained so much weight he had to sit in a wheelchair.

"Perry Mason" was set in a large city populated almost entirely by morons. For example, the prosecutor, Hamilton Burger, was so stupid that the people he prosecuted were always innocent. I mean *always*. I imagine that whenever Hamilton arrested a suspect, the suspect heaved a sigh of relief and hugged his family, knowing he would soon be off the hook.

Now you'd think that after a while Hamilton would have realized he couldn't prosecute his way out of a paper bag, and would have gone into some more suitable line of work, such as sorting laundry. But he kept at it, week after week and year after year, prosecuting innocent people. Nevertheless, everything worked out, because in this particular city the criminals turned out to be even stupider than Hamilton: they always came to the trials, and, after sitting quietly for about twenty minutes, lurched to their feet and confessed. The result was that Perry Mason got a reputation as a brilliant defense attorney, but the truth is that anyone with the intelligence of a can of creamed corn would have looked brilliant in this courtroom.

The major problem with "Perry Mason" is that it is unrealistic: Perry Mason and Hamilton Burger usually speak in understandable English words, and by the time the trial is over everybody has a pretty good grasp of the facts of the case. In real life, of course, lawyers speak mostly in Latin, and by the time they're done nobody has the vaguest notion what the facts are. To understand why this is, you have to understand the history of the U.S. legal system.

In the frontier days, our legal system was very simple: if you broke a law, armed men would chase you and beat you up or throw you in jail or hang you; in extreme cases, they would hang you, then beat you up in jail. So everybody obeyed the law, which was easy to do, because basically there were only two laws:
• No assaulting people.
• No stealing.

This primitive legal system was so simple that even the public understood it. The trials were simple, too:

SHERIFF: Your Honor, the defendant confessed that he shot his wife dead.

JUDGE: Did he admit it freely, or did you have your horse stand on him first, like last time?

SHERIFF: No, sir. He admitted it freely.

JUDGE: Fair enough. String him up.

The trouble with this system was that it had no room for lawyers. If a lawyer had appeared in a frontier courtroom and started tossing around terms such as "habeas corpus," he would have been shot.

So lawyers, for want of anything better to do, formed legislatures, which are basically organizations that meet from time to time to invent new laws. Before long, the country had scads of laws—laws governing the watering of lawns, laws governing the spaying of dogs, laws governing the production and sale of fudge, and so on—and today nobody has the slightest idea what is legal and what is not. This has led to an enormous demand for lawyers. Lawyers don't understand the legal system any better than the rest of us do, but they are willing to talk about it in an impressive manner for large sums of money. In today's legal system, the frontier murder trial would go like this:

SHERIFF: Your Honor—

DEFENSE ATTORNEY: I object. In his use of the word *your,* the witness is clearly stipulating the jurisprudence of a writ of deus ex machina.

PROSECUTING ATTORNEY: On the contrary. In the case of *Merkle* v. *Barnbuster*, the Court clearly ruled that an ex post facto debenture does not preclude the use of the word *your* in a matter of *ad hoc quod erat demonstrandum.*

DEFENSE ATTORNEY: Oh yeah? Well, *Carthaginia delendo est.*

This goes on for several hours, until everybody has forgotten what the trial was about in the first place and the defendant is able to sneak out of the courtroom, unnoticed.

Into the Round file

I LIKE TO CHEER myself up by pretending that my mail actually screams when I throw it into the wastebasket:

*Dear **MR. BARRY**:*
*You have almost certainly won a trillion dollars. We're dead serious, **MR. BARRY**. We're a gigantic publishing company and we just woke up this morning and we said, "By God, lets send one trillion dollars to **MR. BARRY**, no strings attached." That's just the kind of gigantic publishing company we are. And frankly, **MR. BARRY**, you are under no obligation whatsoever to take a six-week trial subscription to a new magazine called* Photographs of Homes That Are Much Nicer Than Yours, *because all we really want to do, **MR. BARRY**, is send you one trillion*
Aieeeeeeeeeeee

Dear Resident of the 15,924th District:
This is the first of an interminable series of newsletters I'll be sending you at your expense so that you'll have photographs of your representative in Washington representing you by eating breakfast with the President. I recently had an opportunity to exchange views with the President during an informal working orientation breakfast for the 742 new congresspersons, and the President and I agreed that one of the most important issues facing the nation, including the 15,924th district, is mineral resources on the ocean floor. I am pleased to report that I have been appointed to the influential Manganese Subcommittee of the House Special Select

Committee on Grayish-White Metallic Elements, and I'm planning a fact-finding trip to
    Aieeeeeeeeeeee

Dear Friend:
    Every day, all over the world, innocent children with large, soulful eyes are getting terrible diseases. Also, countless furry little endangered species are being dismembered by industrialists wielding chain saws. This is all your fault. So we want you to send some money to
    Aieeeeeeeeeeee

Dear Electric Customer:
    Due to inflation, we have been forced to apply for a rate—No, wait, forget that. We can't use inflation anymore. Uh, let's see—Oh yeah. Due to the fact that our new Harbor Vista nuclear generating plant, if we ever get it finished, may have some piping problems that would cause it to emit a deadly cloud of radioactive gas the size of Canada, we have been forced to apply for a rate increase so we'll be able to afford a really top-notch lawyer with his own jet and everything. We realize that, since we just got a rate increase last week, this may seem
    Aieeeeeeeeeeee

*Dear **MR. BARRY**:*
    In a recent column, you stated that Abraham Lincoln ran the hundred-yard dash in 8.4 seconds, and that ice fishermen have the same average IQ scores as mailboxes. As an avid ice fisherman, and chairman of the History Department at Myron B. Thalmus Junior College, I would like to know where you get your
    Aieeeeeeeeeeee

*Dear **MR. BARRY***
   Really! We mean it! One trillion dol
   Aieeeeeeeeeeeee

*Dear **MR. BARRY**:*
   Unless you're the kind of worthless scum that sat idly by while those thugs beat up that woman in New York some years back, you probably have been giving a lot of thought to your family's financial security. No doubt you have said to yourself countless times, "Sure, I'd love to invest $10,000 or more in Liquidated Option Debenture Fiduciary Instruments of Trust, but I don't know where to mail a certified or cashier's check." Well, your worries are over, because
   Aieeeeeeeeeeeee

Dear Brother Barry:
   As you are no doubt aware, the Reverend Bud Albumen didn't develop one of the fastest-growing evangelical organizations in south central Kentucky just by accident. He developed it by building really top-notch studio facilities. But these facilities cost money, which is why the Lord told the Reverend Albumen to tell you to send in a Love Offering of $13.50 per member of your household, or a special rate of $6.75, which is a 50 percent discount, for children under ten. Just as soon as the Reverend Albumen receives your Love Offering, he will ask the Lord not to bring disease and suffering and mud slides to your home, but remember, he can't do this until he receives your
   No! Not the scissors! Please don't aaarrrgggh

Dear Reader:

I hope you enjoyed reading this Large Print book. If you are interested in reading other Beeler Large Print titles, ask your librarian or write to me at:

Thomas T. Beeler, *Publisher*
Post Office Box 659
Hampton Falls, New Hampshire 03844

You can also call me at 1-800-818-7574 and I will send you my latest catalogue.

Traci Wason and I choose the titles I publish in Large Print. Our aim is to provide good books by outstanding authors—books we both enjoyed reading and liked well enough to want to share. We warmly welcome any suggestions for new titles and authors.

Sincerely,